Who Cares?

DR. LYNN JOHNSON

Who Cares?

Copyright © 2024 by Dr. Lynn Johnson. All rights reserved.

All rights reserved. No part of this publication may be reproduced, distributed, or transmitted in any form or by any means, including photocopying, recording, or other electronic or mechanical methods, without the prior written permission of the author, except in the case of brief quotations embodied in critical reviews and certain other noncommercial uses permitted by United States of America copyright law. For permission requests, write to the author at the address below:

www.IamDrLynn.com

Book Cover by: Derek L. Parks

ISBN: 978-1-949562-25-5
LCCN: 2024908877

First Edition: 2024

Printed and bound in the Lakeland, Florida
United States of America.

DEDICATION

Dedicated to the compassionate leaders whose wisdom and mentorship have profoundly influenced the narrative of this book. Your exemplary guidance and genuine care have left an indelible mark on my journey as a leader.

To my beloved family, you are my rock and my inspiration. LyVonski, your love and encouragement fuel my spirit every day. Wynter, Justyce, and Bryndan, your presence brings joy and purpose to my life. And to my precious grandchildren, Carter Lynn, Riley Rae, and Kamry Luella, you are the embodiment of hope and promise for the future.

To my beloved mother-in-law, though you are no longer with us in body, your spirit continues to inspire me every day. From the moment you walked into my life, you have always been in my corner, seeing more in me than I saw in myself. Your belief in me continues to fuel my journey as a leader, and for that, I am eternally grateful.

Thank you for being my constant source of strength and for believing in me, even when I doubted myself. This book is dedicated to each of you, with boundless love and gratitude.

Who Cares?

Foreword   7
Introducing The Cares Framework   13

C - Connection   23

    What Is Connection?   27
    The Benefits   32
    Where Does Connection Begin?   33
    How To Connect   35
    Put It In Action   39

A - Acknowledgment   47

    What Is Acknowledgment?   50
    Acknowledgment Begins With Empathy   54
    How To Make Acknowledgment A Habit   60
    Put It In Action   65

R - Respect   73

    What Is Respect?   75
    Respect Is Not   78
    Why Is Respect Important?   79
    The First Step   82
    Put It In Action   87

E - Empower   97

Authenticity Defined	99
To Be Or Not To Be Authentic	100
What Makes People Conform	103
The Benefits Of Authenticity	107
A Leader's Role In Authenticity	110
The Challenges	111
A Leader's Path In Creating A Culture Of Authenticity	112
Put It In Action	*115*

S - Support   123

Supportive Leadership Defined	126
The Power Of Your Words	129
The Challenges	132
The Need For Supportive Leadership	134
Keys To Develop Supportive Leadership	136
Put It In Action	*141*

Conclusion	151
About The Author	155
Acknowledgments	157
End Notes	159

Foreword

In the world of disconnected work relationships, scattered teams, and employee skepticism, *Who Cares* sets the example for today's leaders. Just as Dr. Lynn Johnson found mentors and leadership examples over the years, we need to seek out our own guides.

When managers do not connect with their teams, the results range from missed opportunities to outright team disfunction. I served on non-profit boards as President of SHRM Jacksonville (2015-2016) and President of HR Florida State Council (2021-2022). I regularly advise presidents and CEOs of small to mid-sized businesses to help them decrease turnover, increase productivity, and improve communication. In my work and service, I help people adapt when conflict occurs and implement tools to enhance team dynamics. Lynn's work provides a template for leaders to follow and outlines a direct path to their success.

Through my experience helping managers connect and engage with their teams, I've seen many try and fail to become the leader they imagined. However, I've also seen leaders succeed and grow an organization that is fully committed to their leadership. What's the difference? Dr. Lynn Johnson has captured the essence of their success in two words... *Who Cares?*

Whether your focus is on retaining talent or you are just trying to make this leadership thing more efficient, take time to journey through the five elements of a **CARES** leader. We know what we're supposed to do, but knowing and doing are two different things! *Who Cares* walks us through:

- Connection
- Acknowledgment
- Respect
- Empower
- Support

Lynn's life experience in both corporate and educational settings has taught her many lessons she shares through personal and relatable stories.

She breaks down each component of a **CARES** leader to help you improve your relationship with your team. Her real world examples and practical steps help us understand the "why" of the **CARES** philosophy. Additionally, Lynn encourages readers to take it beyond learning and provides a path to put it in action.

If you're new to leadership, this book will help you set the foundation for your relationship with your teams. If you're an experienced leader, Lynn's guide will help you identify how to engage more effectively and make a bigger organizational impact.

We learn through trial and error, and when I look over my career and the teams I have led, I realize the mistakes I made and the opportunities I missed to make a difference. Having a resource like *Who Cares* would have been a great asset at the beginning of my leadership journey but will also shape me as a seasoned HR professional.

Foreword

For leaders, the **CARES** model provides a guide through the trials of a rapidly changing leadership landscape. Amid the demographic, generational, and social diversity of today's workplace, take the time to ask *Who Cares* – and transform your team.

Who Cares you ask? You should because your employees do!

Chad V. Sorenson, SHRM-SCP, SPHR
President, Adaptive HR Solutions
Past President, HR Florida State Council

"LEADERSHIP IS NOT ABOUT BEING IN CHARGE.
LEADERSHIP IS ABOUT TAKING CARE OF
THOSE IN YOUR CHARGE."

SIMON SINEK

Introduction

Two words lay hidden in the heart of many employees. They are asking: "Who cares?" This silent question echoes through the corridors of our workplaces around the world. And while it may seem rhetorical, these simple words highlight a deep yearning that most of us are looking for.

We crave a sense of belonging, a fulfillment of purpose, and a workplace that fosters a culture of care—for us. Yet with deadlines, targets, and profits looming heavily in the relentless pursuit of success, this question gets lost. Amid that noise, however, there are leaders who dare to answer it and meet it with intentional action—to help their teams thrive.

These leaders are the ones who hold the key to unlocking untapped potential.

"Who cares?" not answered with a slogan, company picnic, or mission/vision/values painted on the wall. Instead, answering it means attending to the unarticulated. It is our responsibility, as leaders, to go into those spaces.

Who Cares?

Our people wonder:

- Does my well-being matter?
- Do my efforts make a difference?
- Does my leader value me?
- Will my voice be heard, or am I a face in the crowd?
- Does leadership have our interests in mind?
- What if I need more time?
- Will I get support if I ask for it?
- Do I matter?
- Do they even *care*?

They seek answers to these questions because they are fundamental to their sense of belonging, value, and support within the organization. And beneath the surface of our day-to-day operations, you are answering these questions—whether intentional or not.

And the way you answer them hold potential to shape a company's destiny. If these unknowns are left unanswered or dismissed as irrelevant, there is significant data to show this is a guaranteed way to create disengagement, burnout, and a lack of commitment among employees.

A recent Gallup study found that employees who felt strongly that their employers cared about their overall wellbeing are:

- 69% less likely to actively search for a new job
- 71% less likely to report experiencing a lot of burnout
- 5X more likely to strongly advocate for their company as a place to work and to strongly agree they trust the leadership of their organization
- 3X more likely to be engaged at work
- 36% more likely to be thriving in their overall lives[1]

Introduction

The study further found that teams whose members felt more positive about their well-being had better results in customer engagement, profitability, productivity, turnover, and safety.

In my 20+ years of leading teams, I have strived to be a leader who includes the "Who cares?" factor into my leadership philosophy. But I have also felt the pressure of deadlines and demands from my superiors and I've made mistakes. I have witnessed the unarticulated "Who cares?" look in my team members eyes. I have seen a room glaze over as I excitedly shared direction and vision—and it is ill received because I forgot to include *how* my initiative demonstrated care and value, instead of just take more out of my team.

I am not perfect. None of us are. But we do have an opportunity to seek connection and demonstrate that we actually care.

After all, I know what it is like to search for it.

My "Who cares?" quest started at an early age. At five years old, my world changed dramatically when my siblings and I were taken away from our single mother and placed in foster care. That instability planted uncertainty and confusion in my heart that would pervade into my adulthood.

It bothered me that my mother lived in the same city as me, mere miles away, but didn't care enough to be present in my life. Despite being adopted by my grandmother several months later, the haunting scars of abandonment and questions about parental care remained in the background of my mind.

These early experiences showed me firsthand about the profound impact that the lack of care and support can have on a person's life. My perception of the world was shaped by the "Who cares?" question as I matured. In the quest to answer it, this made me empathetic to others' struggles, along with a desire to understand the transformational power of genuine care and support.

The truth is, my upbringing—and the subsequent questions left answered from it—were not, and are not the responsibility of any of my workforce leadership to answer. Just as it is not your responsibility to be a therapist, counselor, or life coach for your team members.

But I share my background to make the point that every single person, in every desk, in every office has a story.

And while we cannot change the past or heal anyone's inner brokenness—we can be aware of the hidden questions in the room and seek to be leaders who create connection, build trust, empathy, and relatability. Thus, we can ensure that appropriate levels of security are present in our organizations.

Because the truth is: Our people are always going to wonder if we care enough to give them that. And I believe the fact you are reading this book means you do. Therefore, I want to empower you to take action to create that culture.

To be an authentic leader, we must understand what the word care truly means. Authentic leadership comes from a genuine concern or care for others' well-being and growth. Practically, this looks like actively listening to concerns, acknowledging unique challenges, and showing unwavering support during triumphs and trials.

Introduction

Contrary to popular belief, caring is not about superficial gestures or empty words. Creating an authentic and empathetic connection is more important than ticking off a list of tasks.

Care is not a sign of weakness, as some may erroneously believe, but is intentional and hard work. It takes tremendous strength to care in a way which promotes trust, loyalty, and resilience.

How is this accomplished? I use a series of actionable steps via the **CARES** model.

To care, we must:

- Connect
- Acknowledge
- Respect
- Empower
- & Support

CONNECTION means I care enough to invest in what matters to each individual I lead. I lead from the mindset that when I use time, energy, and attention in the lives of my team members—then I strengthen my organization as a whole. I can only provide this from a foundation of connection.

ACKNOWLEDGMENT means I care enough to provide assurance. I dare to both acknowledge the good and praise efforts, while at the same time admitting fears in the room and sort through them with my team.

RESPECT means I care enough to hold each person on my team accountable. We have regular discussions on progress, pitfalls, and what I can do to create an environment of support for them to be successful as they continuously give their 100%.

EMPOWER means I care enough to allow each unique person within my leadership to fully be themselves. They are relaxed enough to know they belong and do not have to conform or perform for me in any area of their identity.

SUPPORT means I care enough to develop potential in my team. I actively seeking ways to pour into their training and development, allowing them to be upcoming leaders who connect, acknowledge, respect, and empower others. Thus, continuing a cycle of legacy.

This framework promotes a full and thriving culture of care which not only benefits the employee but has tremendous impact to the company's ROI. In this age, caring leadership is seen as the most important leadership skill, and here's why:

People are struggling, especially workers:

MIT reports that 81% of workers have stress or mental health problems.[2] That's more than 8 out of 10 workers who sit at our table. If leaders don't help the individuals who are running their businesses with these issues, other companies might. Since 81% of people will seek mental health help in the future, it is up to us to put ourselves on their team—and retain good talent in the process.

These challenges harm work performance:

MIT also reports that mental health and burnout problems affect 68% of workers every day.[3] Supported employees are more likely to be committed (63%) and energetic (80%). Additionally, organizations that focus on wellness do better. Practically, this means they have 11x lower absentee rates, 3x higher retention rates, and 2x more

Introduction

chances of beating their financial goals. In a remote work setting, these challenges can be exacerbated due to the lack of face-to-face interaction and the blurred boundaries between work and personal life. Leaders who prioritize caring leadership in remote work environments can help mitigate these challenges by providing support, flexibility, and resources to help employees maintain their well-being and productivity.

Turnover Is Directly Affected:

Struggles make people less engaged and less productive. This leads to employee turnover, which costs companies 50% to 200% of a position's salary. These statistics were made evident during The Great Resignation, which emphasized the fact workers will leave jobs when they don't sense care.

Leaders Are Essential:

Forbes reports that leaders are more important than apps, classes, or therapy when it comes to helping their employees' mental health.[4] The UKG Workforce Institute found that managers have a bigger effect on workers' mental health than therapists or partners.[5]

Most Leaders Don't Have The Tools:

Even though they care, leaders are slow to take action. Research reports that 93% of managers are aware that their employees' mental health effects productivity, but less than a third of them are ready to take action.[6] Many managers report a fear of saying the wrong thing, which could negatively impact participation *and* the bottom line.

But Here Is The Reality:

Leaders who care positively impact revenue—all while creating meaningful connection, which brings fulfillment to both parties.

This level of employee engagement leads to teams which are more motivated, productive, and dedicated to the organization's goals. Such an alignment of values fuels motivation in employees, pushing them to go the extra mile in order to contribute to the company's success. Your care of them develops their care in the company—thus propelling both individual and organization into greater potential for success.

To me, "Who cares?" is more than a simple question; it's a lifelong journey to understand empathy, compassion, and the importance of leaders who genuinely care for those they lead. And I invite you to come with me on this quest to answer a prevailing question that is likely lingering in your team's mind.

"GREAT LEADERS FIND WAYS TO CONNECT WITH THEIR PEOPLE AND HELP THEM FULFILL THEIR POTENTIAL."

STEVEN J. STOWELL

Connection

At the core of human interaction lies a profound concept: Connection. It's the invisible thread that weaves relationships together, builds trust, and shapes our understanding of what it means to leave a legacy through care.

If you were to ask me the first time that connection changed my life, I would have to tell you about my husband. Only, he wasn't my husband at the time. Well—it is about my husband and two chicken wings and a biscuit.

Before we were married, some of the earliest memories I have of us as we were getting to know each other was all of the times he used to pick me up from school and take me to lunch at Kentucky Fried Chicken. We always ordered to go and ate at home. Without fail, he always asked me what my grandmother, who raised me, would like to eat with us. That was an easy answer: two chicken wings and a biscuit.

Who Cares?

Such a simple order might have seemed trivial, but when I look back, I realize that my husband understood what connection meant. He not only mentally comprehended it, but he acted on it—even though there was no additional benefit for him.

He recognized that being with me went far beyond me—it meant entering my world.

He understood that connection included my grandmother, the upbringing I had, and the values instilled in me from my life experiences. His gesture wasn't a mere act of companionship; it was a conscious effort to bridge the gap between his world and mine and to honor the tradition of my grandmother's old-school values.

Think about it. We didn't just stow away and date at restaurants. He was unafraid to step into my home, sit on my couch, and engage in conversations that were more than just small talk. Through his intentional connection, he made an effort to know me, to understand my family, and to build memories which were both genuine and meaningful. This ultimately set the stage for our relationship, but also provided a clear picture of how to care via connection. And it all began with two chicken wings and a biscuit.

You may be thinking, why have we detoured to talk about KFC and courtship? Because we have all encountered small, seemingly insignificant moments when someone went beyond the surface, forging a true bond with us, and perhaps even extend that care to those closest to you. For me, it was with my husband and how he expanded his care of me to my grandmother. For you, you may have experienced something similar from a variety of people in your life. And we can each take an important lesson away from that.

Chapter 1 - Connection

These experiences etch themselves into our memory and shape our perception of caring leadership. Intrinsically, we know that leadership is about far more than directives and charts. It starts there. After all, structure and processes are good. We are all here to do a job and need clear objectives.

But in the process of acting on those goals—a leader who cares is one who genuinely connects and invests in the growth and well-being of each individual on their team.

Such intangibles ripple beyond the immediate task at hand. They resonate deeply with our team members to build trust, form relatability, and instill legacy. Just as someone's investment in you left an indelible mark, so too can our actions echo in the hearts of those we lead.

Connection, as we have defined it inside of the **CARES** framework, embodies the essence of investing in the well-being and growth of each individual led. It signifies a genuine commitment to understanding their aspirations, concerns, and unique perspectives.

By prioritizing connection, leaders demonstrate that they genuinely care about their team's success and fulfillment, fostering a sense of belonging and loyalty within the team. This investment of time, energy, and attention not only strengthens individual relationships but also enriches the collective fabric of the organization.

Increasingly, employees are demanding connection in the workplace. In the wake of the "Great Resignation" or the "Great Disconnection" phenomenon, where many employees have left their jobs in search of better opportunities or improved work-life balance, research has proven that building real connections at work is crucial. Team members in every organization have options. As individuals reassess their career priorities, many are seeking roles that align with their values. Companies which prioritize authentic relationships along with promoting communication channels in which team members feel valued, understood, and connected are more likely to retain them. There is more to the Great Resignation than simply leaving a job. Employees are searching for environments that offer meaning and belonging.

Research reports that 71% of executives have stated that engaged, connected employees are essential to their success.[7] This is positive. But there is a missing link when it comes to taking action on this knowledge. According to a 2023 study by Eagle Hill Consulting, 45% of U.S. workers perceive that their employers are not adequately investing in initiatives which promote employee connection.[8]

This observation sheds light on a critical gap between employee expectations and organizational actions. Such findings emphasize the need for decision makers in each company to prioritize strategies that enhance relational bonds within their workforce. This is critical—and must occur at all levels.

When connection is missing, you are more likely to find disengaged employees—and disengaged employees stall the process when it comes to completing goals. So, what creates this chasm between leadership and front line, direct reports and supervisors? Red Thread Research and Enboarder conclude that the top two barriers to connection in the workplace include the fact that managers are not providing enough support (29%) and that managers/leaders not providing enough transparency in decisions (26%).[9] The good news is that both of these are overcome when we are intentional and take action to care.

Chapter 1 - Connection

WHAT IS CONNECTION?

Before we dive further in the concept of *how* to connect, let's define what it is and isn't.

To me, connection is an artful fusion that looks beyond the surface. It takes us into the complexities of what makes us human. When we feel connected to another person, this has built up from more than just a few casual exchanges or interactions. It's an intricate dance of getting to know someone for who they are *at their core*. To truly understand someone, we must peer beyond the façade, embrace their quirks, and understand how their life experiences have molded them into the unique individual they are. This is true, no matter the type of relationship.

Within the workplace, forging connections may appear complex. Balancing personal and professional boundaries can be challenging. Yet, it is not impossible. Careful, yes. But certainly doable. The core principle remains the same. Authentic connections are built on understanding what is important to another person—and bringing value to it. This can only occur if we dig deeper than surface-level exchanges.

Abraham Maslow's Hierarchy of Needs Theory proves to be a powerful framework to unpack how connection meets the needs which lie within every individual. To go one step deeper, I want to use it to dive into the complicated relationship between individual well-being and workplace satisfaction.

Maslow's model helps us to visualize our desires, needs, and what makes us tick. As we move upwards through the chart, we have an opportunity to hit what I call the sweet spot of "love and belonging." This stage emphasizes our need for meaningful interactions, shared experiences, and belonging. It proves that feeling a secure sense of care allows an individual to reach "self-actualization" in which they are able to reach full potential. But to achieve this, love and belonging must be present first.

This desire for social connection is deeply rooted in our evolutionary history. Humanity has evolved as inherently social beings who thrive on collaboration, support, and sharing. Thus, authentic human connections contribute significantly to our overall sense of fulfillment and happiness, thus enriching our lives.

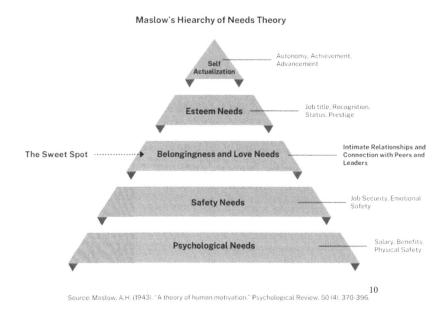

Source: Maslow, A.H. (1943). "A theory of human motivation." Psychological Review, 50 (4), 370-396. [10]

When I take Maslow's concept and filter it through the lens of connection in the workplace, I see four specific ways that we can practically move toward leading ourselves and our teams towards self-actualization.

Chapter 1 - Connection

We reach it through:

Genuine Bonds:

In the workplace, genuine bonds tie individuals together, mirroring their importance in our personal lives. A foundation of trust equips teams to maneuver through setbacks or scale as well as obstacles or objectives. When leaders and coworkers truly understand, value, and support one another, they know how to weather the storms or tackle new risks. This trust serves as a driving force for team efforts, open dialogue, and teamwork. This collectively drives productivity to greater heights.

Unity-Building:

Imagine a workplace in which every team member contributed to a larger, interconnected tapestry. An organization that fosters an environment of connection is unstoppable. Through inclusivity and by nurturing each person's unique skill set— we find that employee job satisfaction has room to flourish. In such an environment, ideas are freely shared, support is readily available, and collaborative successes are commonplace.

Connecting And Thriving:

Maslow reminds us that realizing our potential is dependent upon our ability to interact with others. The well-being of an employee is fundamentally linked to the quality of their workplace connections. Organizations that value relationship, and provide pathways to foster it, cultivate a culture of contentment and satisfaction within its workforce, resulting in happier, more engaged employees.

Building Commitment:

Picture a workplace alive with tangible connections, where colleagues aren't just coworkers, but allies. In such an environment, the "office" feels like home. It ignites commitment and motivates employees. When employees feel as if their effort, energy, and ideas are truly part of the organization, they willingly invest. This leads individuals to find a sense of purpose within their interconnected work community. Not only are the people within our workspaces fulfilled—it also results in increased productivity and reduced turnover, which benefit the company.

Creating cultures in which it is possible to achieve fulfillment is crucial. Will it require more from us, as leaders? Absolutely. This is not easy. Many of us are accountable to our own executive leaders. We are aware of the objectives we have been asked to complete. And creating room for intangibles such as self-actualized employees or fulfilled teams is not always on the quarterly report.

I would dare to call us to spend time on the intangibles. Without connection, we run the risk of creating an environment marked by disengagement, distrust, and dwindling morale. This detachment which ensues can spiral into reduced productivity, lackluster performance, and an increased likelihood of turnover. We know that this is not the outcome we want, so in order to proceed, we must define what connection is not.

Connection Is Not Surface-Level:

Real connection is a complex phenomenon that extends past surface-level interactions. It's a relationship fostered by acceptance and trust which is felt by both parties. When individuals genuinely understand each other's opinions, attitudes, and objectives—a deep bond develops—allowing for an ease of communication. In turn, this promotes a deeper appreciation for each party's contribution. Both people have confidence that their bond can withstand difficulties and uncertainties because they have achieved this level of honesty.

Connection Is Not Transactional:

Although activities and goals are essential to the workplace, genuine connection goes beyond task fulfillment alone. It involves an emotional give-and-take versus a transactional exchange of favors. Authentic connection piques interest in the other person beyond the function they play, or what we can "get out of them." Instead, it develops relational capital that brings value to both sides.

Connection Is Not Forced:

Genuine connections cannot be forced or manufactured. It must develop naturally. This may prove to be frustrating for achievement-oriented leaders and personalities which are driven. But it can be fostered, even if it is not an inherent mindset. No matter our personality, we build connection when we allow natural interactions infused with care to occur via curiosity and a commitment to promote the good of others. They naturally arise when people have common values, experiences, or objectives.

Forced conversations with checklists and ticking interactions are not caring. Instead, sincere connections develop because of common interests, shared objectives, and a shared desire to grow and learn from one another.

Connection Is Not One-Sided:

Relationship takes us beyond titles or hierarchal positions. Regardless of rank, when connection is present—engagement is reciprocal. The impact is felt by both parties. A two-way street approach encourages candid communication, open ideation, and teamwork. This enables comprehensive growth and advancement for individuals and the organization as a whole.

Connection Is Not Manipulative:

Genuine relationship is free of manipulation and covert goals. It is rooted from sincerity, empathy, and a genuine concern for other people's welfare. Such connection lacks hidden agendas or manipulative strategies which could destroy trust.

Connection Is Not Ignoring Boundaries:

Though connection is about bringing individuals together, it's still vital for all parties to maintain respect for personal boundaries. Healthy connection respects each person's space and comfort levels. It fosters an atmosphere in which people may interact and communicate without fear of exposure or feeling uncomfortable. Understanding and respecting appropriate restrictions elevates a relationship's integrity while promoting safety at work.

THE BENEFITS

There are many benefits to making meaningful connections at work, such as:

- **Greater Employee Satisfaction:** Employees are happier with their jobs and have better morale when they feel connected to their coworkers, supervisors, and the company's mission.
- **Increased Loyalty And Engagement:** Meaningful connections create a feeling of community and belonging, which make employees more loyal to the company and more interested in their work.

- **Better Communication And Teamwork:** Making real connections with other people on your team makes it easier for them to converse and work together, which encourages creativity, innovation, and problem-solving.

- **Positive Work Environment:** Making important connections at work makes everyone feel valued, respected, and understood, which leads to a positive and supportive work environment.

To build a supportive and engaged workforce, leaders need to understand the value of important connections and put plans in place to encourage them.

WHERE DOES CONNECTION BEGIN?

According to Andrea Couto, VP of solution engineering at Betterworks, "a top reason employees stay—or leave—an organization is tied to their manager relationship." Managers, she argues, will need to become "highly relational forming connections" based on shared interests and attentive listening.[11]

That being said, when we are looking for an answer to the question, "Where does connection begin?" I would submit to you that it must begin with us.

By prioritizing relationship building inside our teams, we can show that we have a keen awareness of each member's unique requirements. When we lead with compassion and appreciation for one another, we can instill hope in our followers and motivate them to take action. As we foster this mindset, we create a safe place where people feel comfortable making connections that fuel both individuals and lead to a multiplier effect in our organizations.

Personal experience has taught me the value of genuine connection between a leader and their team. In my role, I made it a point to sit down with each member of my team individually on a regular basis to hear about their goals, fears, and struggles. The feedback I was given was eye-opening.

I discovered that several people on the team were struggling to maintain a healthy work-life balance due to lengthy commutes. The daily stress of travel and additional time away from family created a major impact on their motivation and productivity.

Recognizing this as a linchpin issue, I saw the need for a quick fix. I advocated for a schedule that would let my team work from home on certain days. Even though this change was relatively small, it had far-reaching consequences. Reducing their commute increased focus, decreased absenteeism, and increased job satisfaction.

The unquestionable return on investment from my time spent connecting and listening to what everyone on my team valued—yet was lacking—completely shocked me. Together, we underwent a remarkable change. Since they felt seen, heard, and supported they were more engaged, motivated, and productive. This propelled the success of both our team and the company.

Just as sturdy chains are built one link at a time, strong relationships between managers and their team members must develop one interaction at a time. Leaders have power to increase employee engagement and happiness if they are intentional about creating those interactions. Employees are showing us what they value. Belonging is more important than salary these days.

A study by McKinsey & Company found that the top three reasons employees gave for leaving their jobs included not feeling valued by their companies (54%), not feeling like they belonged at work (51%), or not feeling valued by their managers (52%).[12]

This only proves that making the effort to grow those relationships isn't a luxury; it's a priority to our current workforce. And we are in a position to ensure that the individuals within our organizations have what they need.

HOW TO CONNECT

As leaders, we get the privilege of creating a culture that prioritizes genuine interactions and fosters a sense of belonging. And the best part? You have what it takes to start.

Here are seven ways you can start connecting today:

#1 - Be Authentic:

The foundation of lasting connection is authenticity. Be vulnerable and true to yourself as you build relationships with your team. As appropriate, share your personal struggles and experiences with them so they can see the human side of you. Spend time actively hearing their viewpoint without passing judgment or barking a quick fix. We have what it takes to foster an atmosphere of openness and trust by being sincere.

Try this:

- Where applicable, talk about your personal growth experience, the difficulties you've encountered, and how you overcame them.
- To build a sense of togetherness, encourage team members to share their unique experiences and tales during team meetings, including wins.
- Create personal ties by talking to others during breaks and mealtimes about activities outside of work that you both enjoy doing.

#2 - Be Empathetic:

Empathy creates a link between people which allows them to meet each other on a deeper level. Consider the thoughts and feelings of your staff. Be kind and helpful when personal challenges surface.

Recognize and validate their feelings and give them a secure environment in which to express themselves.

Try this:

- Set up routine, one-on-one check-ins to talk about personal and work-related issues in a private, compassionate setting.
- Provide time-off alternatives or flexible work schedules to employees who are experiencing personal difficulties.
- Develop a culture of mutual respect and support by holding workshops or training sessions focused on mental health, wellness, and empathy.

#3 - Be Safe:

Open dialogue and engagement naturally surface from secure atmospheres. Establish a culture where employees can voice their thoughts without fear of repercussion. Set a good example by being open to feedback and acknowledging your limitations.

Try this:

- Implement an anonymous feedback system to allow staff to voice ideas or grievances while protecting their identities.
- Address faults in an honest and open manner. Vocalize personal lessons learned. This demonstrates that it is okay to admit mistakes and grow from them.
- Create psychological safety during team meetings by encouraging diverse viewpoints and acknowledging every contribution.

Chapter 1 - Connection

#4 - Be Intentional:

Making meaningful connections requires initiative and effort. Engaging with employees means moving conversation beyond their tasks. Take time for informal discussions and team-building exercises.

Regularly convey your appreciation for their time and for their personal contributions.

Try this:

- Plan recurring team-building activities or online gatherings to help workers connect and get to know one another better.
- Allocate time in team meetings for non-work-related discussions such as life updates and personal wins.
- Create opportunities for employees to meet with a mentor or coach who will develop them both professionally and personally.

#5 - Be Random:

Spontaneity infuses joy into the workplace and builds relationships via shared experiences. Surprise your staff with thoughtful acts. These unplanned events generate enduring memories and improve interpersonal bonds.

Try this:

- Send customized, handwritten cards of appreciation to staff members as a way of acknowledging their efforts and commitment, both large and small.
- Establish rapport by hosting unplanned coffee breaks or online conversations to catch up on *non* work-related issues.
- Surprise team members with small tokens of appreciation on special days, such as birthdays, project completion dates, and work anniversaries.

#6 - Be Honest:

Always tell the truth; it's the best policy for maintaining healthy relationships. Communicate openly about progress and setbacks. Leaders who are honest and open with their teams are highly valued, especially when being transparent about challenges.

Try this:

- Communicate the company's goals and seasonal struggles in order to keep the team focused on the present.
- When you make a mistake, own up to it and explain what action you intend to implement to fix it.
- Provide employees with honest feedback, highlighting both areas for improvement and praising accomplishments.

#7 - Be Supportive:

A leader who is supportive builds rapport with their team by actively assisting individuals in achieving their goals. By providing direction and support, you empower them to flourish.

Try this:

- Facilitate staff growth and career progression through mentoring programs.
- Give workers the chance to advance their careers in ways that coincide with their own personal skill set and desires.
- Reinforce employees' worth to the company by recognizing and celebrating their successes.

Chapter 1 - Connection

PUT IT IN ACTION
EMPLOYEE CONNECTION WORKSHEET

Reflection And Self-Awareness

1. Reflect on your own leadership style: How do you currently connect with your employees? What strategies have you used to foster meaningful connections?
2. Self-awareness check: How well do you understand your own strengths, weaknesses, and challenges in connecting with others? What one thing do you do well? What one area do you want to develop in?
3. Consider your past experiences: Recall a time when a leader's connection positively impacted your work experience. How did it make you feel? What specific actions did the leader take that spoke to you?
4. Gather insights from others through 360 feedback: Seek input from colleagues, direct reports, and supervisors on your leadership style and how effectively you connect with others. What are your strengths in building connections, and where do you have opportunities for growth?

Building Genuine Connections

1. Be Genuine: List three ways you can show authenticity in your interactions with employees.

    Example: Share a personal anecdote or challenge during team meetings to establish relatability.

2. Be Empathetic: Identify two ways you can demonstrate empathy and support for employees facing challenges.

   Example: Schedule regular one-on-one meetings to provide a confidential space for employees to share their concerns.

3. Be Safe: Describe how you currently create a safe environment for open communication and employee feedback.

   Example: Implement an anonymous platform for employees to share their thoughts without fear of repercussions.

Nurturing Intentional Connections

1. Be Intentional: List three ways you can allocate time for non-work interactions and team-building activities.

   Example: Plan a quarterly team outing to encourage relationship-building.

2. Be Random: Brainstorm ideas for unexpected gestures that show employees you care.

   Example: Host impromptu virtual coffee breaks to catch up with team members on personal topics.

   Bonus: Offer to bring them their favorite coffee.

3. Be Honest: Describe how you currently provide transparent communication to your team.

   Example: Share both company successes and challenges during your next team meeting to foster trust and credibility.

Chapter 1 - Connection

4. Be Supportive: Identify three ways you can actively support employees in their professional growth.

   Example: Offer mentorship opportunities to develop skills and advance team members careers.

Action Steps

1. Choose one strategy from each category (Genuine, Sympathetic, Safe, Intentional, Random, Honest, & Supportive) to implement within the next month.
2. Set specific goals for these actions, including how often you'll engage in them and the expected outcomes.
3. Determine how you will measure the impact of your connection efforts. Will you use feedback, employee surveys, or other methods?
4. Create a timeline for reviewing and adjusting your connection strategies based on the results you observe.
5. Choose an accountability partner: Select someone you trust and respect, whether it's a colleague, mentor, or friend, to regularly check in with you on your progress with implementing your chosen connection strategies. This person can offer support, encouragement, and feedback to help you stay on track and make adjustments as needed.

Remember, the goal is to cultivate authentic and meaningful connections that contribute to a positive workplace culture and foster employee engagement. Use this worksheet as a guide to continuously enhance your leadership approach through the lens of the **CARES** Framework.

Who Cares?

Chapter 1 - Connection

"APPRECIATION CAN MAKE A DAY, EVEN CHANGE A LIFE.
YOUR WILLINGNESS TO PUT IT INTO WORDS
IS ALL THAT IS NECESSARY."

MARGARET COUSINS

Acknowledgment 2

I began my professional journey fresh out of high school. I was fortunate to land a job at a small insurance company in my hometown. I saw this opportunity as a beacon. I knew this would guide me toward my ultimate dream job with a prestigious insurance company. Excitement flowed through my veins as I started a new chapter.

But life had other plans.

Only months after starting my position, I found out I was expecting my first child. The first trimester brought typical morning sickness, but day-by-day it got worse. When I spoke with my girlfriends about my experience, I realized my symptoms went beyond a normal pregnancy. Instead, I faced severe nausea, uncontrollable vomiting, and was faint or dizzy at the slightest movement.

I struggled with my tasks at work each day. I wanted to be present. I wanted to give back to a company who had given me such a great role. But I didn't know what to do. Leaving work one day, I felt a rush of dizziness and almost fainted. I knew I had to get help.

Heading to the doctors, I was diagnosed with *hyperemesis gravidarum*. The baby was okay. And my symptoms would fade without hurting my pregnancy—but the prognosis was not good for me and my working world for the next several weeks and months.

Lying in bed that night, a whirlwind of thoughts consumed me. *Should I quit? Would they let me go if I told them what was going on? What do I do?*

My biggest fear was losing the job I had worked so hard for. I didn't want to ruin my career right as I began it. Despite the relentless sickness, I persevered. I showed up to work every day and navigated the constant trips to the bathroom and rushing nausea. I committed to myself that as long as I was not putting my pregnancy in risk in any way that I could "suck it up." I would just have to power through. I figured it was the cost of trying to be a mom and a career woman. I just had to keep going.

But that is when care changed the game for me. Here is where Bobby and Renee, my immediate managers, became my lifelines.

One day, as I sat at my desk with head and stomach whirling, I swore to myself that I could be productive—despite how I felt.

To this day, I wonder what I looked like.

Renee took the seat beside me, and I could feel myself stiffen. I had tried too hard for no one to notice, but I was sure she was going to reprimand me. With a firm and yet soft tone, she asked the question that had haunted me: "Why do you come to work feeling this way?"

My heart raced. I was convinced my termination was imminent. But I realized Renee's question was filled with an authentic inquiry and a genuineness that I hadn't expected.

Chapter 2 – Acknowledgment

Care met me where I was at.

"Our whole team is here for you," she said gently. "We want you to know that we're here to support you and your new family."

I felt the fact that she cared for me wash over me and I exhaled a breath I had been holding onto since I saw those pink lines on my pregnancy test.

I mustered the courage to explain my fears about my job security, my doubts about my productivity, and my concern that I had not been seen as an asset in my current state. In response, she reassured me that they would help me through such a challenging time and were open to finding ways for me to still contribute to the company, while also caring for myself.

Do you know what happened to my fear of being fired? Renee swept it away with a short check-in conversation and a simple reassurance: "Lynn, that's not going to happen."

She reminded me of the quality of my work, praised my potential, and assured me that this temporary setback wouldn't alter her view of the outstanding employee I was.

The conversation took less than fifteen minutes. Yet, it alleviated months of fear, all because my manager was unafraid to address the unspoken worry I had been too afraid to utter. And in doing so, she not only brought relief to my present, but she also locked in my loyalty for the future.

As leaders, you may not encounter an employee with *hyperemesis gravidarum*. But everyone has something that keeps them awake at night—something which is impacting their work world.

If you are lucky to have a moment in which it is appropriate to tackle it with them, you can help them to find victory in their own personal battles and let them know that you care. In turn, you just might slay the unspoken fears that are holding them back from their optimal performance.

Does it take work? Absolutely. But as we continue to answer the question "Who cares?" we develop stronger teams, and ultimately stronger organizations. A leader's ability to pause and acknowledge when challenges are present in their employees' lives, while also addressing their uncertainties around them, is a testament to true leadership.

To unpack "the how" of acknowledgment—let's return to the **CARES** framework.

WHAT IS ACKNOWLEDGMENT?

- Acknowledgment means I care enough to provide assurance. I dare to acknowledge the good and praise efforts, while at the same time admitting fears in the room and sort through them with my team.

After all, our teams are looking to us for that sense of validation. And it is our responsibility to make sure they have it.

In Oprah Winfrey's powerful speech for the 2013 Harvard Commencement Ceremony, she encapsulated humanity's search to be acknowledged and the fact it transcends the boundaries of fame, status, and circumstance.

"I have to say that the single most important lesson I learned in 25 years talking every single day to people was that there's a common denominator in our human experience.... The common denominator that I found in every single interview is we want to be

Chapter 2 – Acknowledgment

validated. We want to be understood. I've done over 35,000 interviews in my career. And as soon as that camera shuts off, everyone always turns to me and inevitably, in their own way, asks this question: "Was that, OK?" I heard it from President Bush. I heard it from President Obama. I've heard it from heroes and from housewives. I've heard it from victims and perpetrators of crimes. I even heard it from Beyoncé in all of her Beyoncé-ness .... [We] all want to know one thing: "Was that OK?" "Did you hear me?" "Do you see me?" "Did what I say mean anything to you?"[13]

The desire for acknowledgment is going to be preset in every meeting you lead, each goal you set for your employees, and every single project you oversee.

As Oprah highlights, this yearning for validation is about recognizing the shared humanity in all of us. It's about acknowledging each person's unique journey, whether they are world leaders or everyday heroes—and assuring them that their voice matters. It's a response to their contribution which declares values at what they offered and says, "I see you. I hear you. Your story is important, and it has touched me."

In short, it shows you cared.

Acknowledgment is a powerful way to remember how linked we all are, which helps build a sense of unity and shared humanity. When we notice other people, we see the thing that brings us all together, despite our differences. All of us want the same basic human relationship and understanding from each other. Acknowledgment is a powerful reminder of that. It isn't just a surface-level act; it's a recognition of the deeper parts of our shared existence that show how important empathy and kindness are in the way we interact with each other.

This idea fits perfectly with the second pillar of the **CARES** Framework, which stresses how important recognition is for creating a caring and helpful workplace. When people are recognized for their achievements and hard work in their jobs, it creates a positive environment that encourages teamwork and mutual respect. It builds a culture at work where people feel valued and appreciated, which gives them a feeling of belonging and drives them to do their best. By incorporating gratitude into leadership, companies can improve relationships between employees, get them more involved in their work, and create a space that cares about their health and growth.

The distinction between recognition and acknowledgment is crucial for us as **CARES** Leaders.

While many companies have recognition rituals—acknowledgment tends to go deeper. Both are powerful, and both are needed.

And yet, at times acknowledgment can be harder to implement.

Generally, recognizing someone means thanking them for something they did and did well. This might happen when someone reaches a goal, does good work, or is consistently on time and leaves a good example for others. It is behaviors based and focuses on performance.

On the other hand, acknowledgment is more specific.

When we acknowledge someone, we don't just point out their deeds; we also show that we like them as a person. Acknowledgment says, "I see you. I see your contribution. I see the value you offer." This might look like complimenting their qualities, pointing out positive characteristics they might not even see in themselves, or sharing how you value what they bring to the team and company as a whole.

In essence, recognition is about what people do, while acknowledgment is about noting and valuing *who they are.*

Chapter 2 - Acknowledgment

Additionally, like Bobby and Renee did for me, acknowledgment enters any struggle and chooses to stand with someone through a challenge. It dares to still say, "I still see you. I understand this is hard. But we still value you."

Both sides of the coin matter. When we engage in this kind of care people feel more connected and appreciated at work.

Recognition, acknowledgment of struggle, and acknowledgment of someone's value each contribute to making the workplace a great place to be and a constant source of motivation.

Practically, these actions can be shown in different ways. It can be as simple as an email or text message, body language, or the words we choose when we answer.

No matter the method, acknowledgment serves as the last part of a full conversation loop.

This loop begins with us paying close attention and ends with an acknowledgment response. Whether it's a thank-you email or a simple "noted" text message, acknowledgment demonstrates care and encourages the recipient's purpose. In turn, this creates connection for them, while making them aware that you see their contribution as important.

Good leaders thank their employees for a good job. Great leaders also describe what it means to them that the job got done. Outstanding leaders uplevel by then sharing their observations.

That is acknowledgment in its core.

As leaders who care, we are able to see each person behind their job titles and recognize their worth as people outside of their jobs. And in doing so, we become stronger leaders who can gain the respect of our teams.

A Harvard study of 14,500 U.S. workers found that employees reach their full potential when "supervisors notice and acknowledge employee feelings, understand how their decisions will affect employees, and help them manage their emotions."

This whole-person method incorporates acknowledgment, meets the emotional needs of employees, and provides them a sense of belonging, purpose, and satisfaction that goes far beyond traditional employee recognition. It's a move toward a society where workers are valued not only for their results but also for how they got there. This makes employees stronger and more driven—which drives our organizations towards success.

ACKNOWLEDGMENT BEGINS WITH EMPATHY

Helice Bridges, known as "Grandma Sparky" for her heartwarming Blue Ribbon Ceremony, gives out blue ribbons which are stamped with the statement "Who I am makes a difference."[15]

The ceremony's simplicity masks its deep effect.

Grandma Sparky says that what really counts is acknowledgment, a moment in which to speak from the heart, make eye contact, and use someone's name. It turns words into a gift that means something. The human to human to connection that she offers each employee during the Blue-Ribbon Ceremony goes beyond a ritual and into a moment of care—and it all begins with empathy.

I have never been the recipient of Grandma Sparky's care, nor have I been handed a prized blue ribbon, but I do know what it is like to feel acknowledged in a moment of connection. When I was pregnant with my first child, Renee didn't give me a blue ribbon. Instead, she

Chapter 2 - Acknowledgment

took the time to empathize with me, provide the comfort I needed, and value my contribution—despite my illness.

To this day, I don't think she knows what she gave me.

As leaders, we don't always realize how important these seemingly small actions can be. Often, our responsibilities keep our focus on the bigger picture of the company. This is good. This is important. It is just unfortunate that it causes us to forget how important these smaller, more personal interactions are.

If I could have any superpower—I would want to have maximized Emotional Intelligence. Emotional intelligence (EI), at its core, is the ability to identify, understand, control, and use one's own emotions and the emotions of others in a way that improves relationships and helps one grow as a person. Thus, I definitely want more of that in my life. This is why I chose it as my superpower! I know an increased EI would help me to acknowledge the individuals within my circle of influence—thus boosting the health of my organization.

Emotionally intelligent leaders are excellent at understanding their feelings and controlling them in appropriate levels. This creates a more peaceful and caring workplace for the leader and their direct reports. But EI goes beyond just the emotions of the leader.

- Leaders with increased EI can identify and understand the emotions of their team members. This paves the way for connected relationships, clear communication, and well-developed teamwork because they are aware of the emotions in the room and can work with them instead of over them.

- Leaders who are emotionally intelligent act with compassion. To be empathetic means putting yourself in someone else's shoes. This becomes a vital skill when making business choices since decisions and outcomes affect people in different ways. Being aware of those and acknowledging them so that each one can be addressed helps to remove obstacles and clear a path for alignment.

- Leaders with EI can read verbal and unconscious cues from coworkers. Since people don't always say what they're feeling, a leader may need to be the first to verbalize objections—allowing others to present their own concerns, criticisms, or ideas. Being aware of those emotions helps everything to be aired in the right spaces, versus morph into hidden grudges or resentment.

Emotional intelligence is fueled by empathy allows leaders to connect with employees on a deeper level, making each person feel like they are respected and understood. In turn, this makes employees feel valued and more likely to be involved.

In a world where problems and challenges are always changing, we need empathic leaders. Yet, there does not seem to be as many as one might think. Which leads me to wonder: *Why do so many leadership models rank confidence and toughness ahead of empathy? And is this why acknowledgment tends to fall to the wayside?*

I see several factors which steal our focus from empathetic acknowledgment:

Chapter 2 - Acknowledgment

- For one, cultural and societal norms play a huge role. Assertiveness, decisiveness, and toughness are highly praised in traditional models of leadership. These traits are perceived as signs of strong and effective leadership, leaving empathy to be perceived as weakness. In turn, emerging leaders may feel as if these are the rules at hand. One might be tempted to believe: *In order to be accepted and respected in my profession, I must use the traditional model to prevail.* But studies are beginning to question if that thought process has created the outcomes those same leaders had hoped to achieve.

- Secondly, many of us face misconceptions about empathy. Some believe that leaders who show empathy are "too soft" or too emotional. This contrasts the idea that leaders should be tough and unbending in order to make hard choices and get things done. These false beliefs block good leaders from developing empathy skills which could make them great leaders. In turn, this can lead to workplaces which lack emotional intelligence and are not perceived as genuine.

- Fear of being weak is the third factor that gets in the way of empathic leadership. For leaders to show empathy, they must risk vulnerability. Let's be honest. There is risk in recognizing our own feelings and then connecting with the feelings of others. Many of us might worry that our vulnerability could be used against us or hurt our influence. This is valid—and yet can be navigated in a way which keeps an environment and our relationships healthy—if we dare to lean into authentic connection.

- Lastly, a constant pressure to perform makes leaders put results ahead of empathy. A laser focus on goals emphasizes a need to be tough and get things done, even if humanity gets sent to the back burner. All of these things make it hard to encourage empathic leadership in the workplace today.

It's important to realize that having empathy and being a great leader are not mutually exclusive. In fact, empathy can increase effectiveness. How? Because empathy makes it easier to communicate, gets employees involved, and improves the overall culture of a company.

When leaders combine empathy with other important leadership traits, they create workplaces that are welcoming, helpful, and successful. To raise a new generation of leaders who can handle the complex problems of our modern world, it's important to rid ourselves of the myths surrounding empathy and focus on its benefits within our own leadership.

While practicing empathy may not always be easy, I firmly believe it's the human and right thing to do. But the question many of us has is: "Where do we begin?" Since empathy is developed and not innate, we must practice.

Here are simple action steps we can take to promote our own EQ and pave the way for empathetic acknowledgment:

Understanding and Validation: To exercise empathy, you must understand the thoughts and feelings of others. This is how leaders demonstrate that they understand their employees' work, problems, and feelings. With this perspective, they are able to validate the experiences and efforts of each person on their team. In turn, acknowledgment shows care for what each employee is going through.

Creating A Supportive Environment:

Empathetic leaders know how to cultivate a supportive and caring place to work. In turn employees who feel cared for and understood are more likely to be motivated to do their best work.

Chapter 2 - Acknowledgment

Building Trust:

Empathy paves the way for leaders and employees to trust each other. When workers feel care from their leaders and know that their personal and professional goals matter, they are more likely to trust leadership's plans and decisions.

Enhancing Emotional Connection:

When leaders and employees acknowledge each other with empathy, a crucial emotional connection is formed. Your appreciation communicates not only thanks, but that you understand the mental journey an employee underwent to get to that point. This emotional link increases happiness, builds motivations, and leaves employees with an increased satisfaction in their roles.

Improving Employee Well-Being:

Empathetic acknowledgment improves our general well-being. Recipients feel respected and understood, which lowers stress and builds emotional fortitude. This, in turn, increases mental health and resiliency for future obstacles.

Empathy is the fuel which powers acknowledgment and recognition. In turn, this encourages loyalty, productivity, and a good atmosphere at work. If we were to be honest, this is something we all long for—no matter what role or title we hold. Yet it is on us, as leaders, to be the ones to initiate it for our organizations.

This is how we show we **CARE**.

HOW TO MAKE ACKNOWLEDGMENT A HABIT

Acknowledging individuals effectively takes a thoughtful and personalized approach. To begin, consider these steps:

Listen With Intent:

Listen to what your employees have to say. Learn about their wants, goals, and problems. This will help you make sure that your acknowledgment of their contribution or your acknowledgment of their struggle will fit their individualized needs and tastes.

Try this:

- Set up regular one-on-one meetings with each employee to talk about their goals, problems, and ideas for improvement. During that time, select at least one action item to implement change together.
- Create an anonymous system for employees to share their thoughts, worries, and ideas. Then, publicly communicate at least one action step that leadership will take to address a single concern.

Make Acknowledgment Personal:

Whenever possible, personalize your thank you. But be wise in your method. Note that some workers like to be recognized in public, while others prefer private recognition. Your **CARE** will have maximum impact if a thank you is offered in the employee's chosen method of communication *and* it fits their personality.

Try this:

- For the introverted employee: Have a private check-in to thank them for their consistent, great work. Be sure to share how important their presence and productivity is to the team.
- For the extroverted employee: Give public praise in team settings which include remarks on their leadership skills and impact to the company.

Be Sincere And Specific:

When you acknowledge an employee, be truthful and clear about what you value about them. Define what they did that you observed and why you think their action or attitude was important. Specific praise exceeds the vague as it indicates that you paid attention to them and their accomplishments.

Try this:

- During a performance review, provide specific examples of what an employee has done well. This might be instances such as meeting tight schedules or bringing in more sales than expected.
- This might sound like, "I really appreciate how carefully you worked on our project. It helped a lot that you paid attention to every detail."

Acknowledge Effort And Progress:

Don't only thank people for big achievements. Even when an employee hasn't hit a specific goal yet, they should be praised for their hard work and progress along the way. This keeps motivation high over long stretch goals. Commenting on how far they've come and how much they've overcome makes an employee feel seen for more than the outcome, but for each step in achieving it.

Try this:

- Even when an employee hasn't reached a goal yet, they should be praised for their commitment to improve their skills.
- Recognize a team member's persistence and tenacity as they trudge through challenging projects. Offer positive comments which highlight how they've grown during the process and why that matters to the company.

Connect Acknowledgment To Organizational Values:

Find ways to acknowledge when team members demonstrate the values and culture of your company. When you appreciate the ways they embody these values, it speaks to how important they are in the workplace.

Try this:

- Example #1: Publicly recognize an employee who handled a tough client situation with honesty and professionalism. Note how this matches the company's core value of integrity. This not only encourages the employee, but also sets the bar for their team.
- Example #2: Privately praise an employee's commitment to source environmentally friendly vendors, even though this took more research and prospecting on their part. Acknowledge that their efforts were directly in line with the organization's values of environmental responsibility.

Promote Self-Care:

Encourage self-care and emphasize the importance of mental, emotional, and physical well-being. Lead by example by caring for yourself with healthy boundaries. Provide resources to support their self-care journeys, and check-in on progress.

Chapter 2 - Acknowledgment

Try this:

- If you are the kind of boss who works seven days a week and answers emails at all hours, realize that you are adding to the stress of your workers. Don't just talk about self-care and forgo modeling it. Set the example on how important it is to take time away from work. Show how it's done. In turn, you will create a culture that supports these goals, giving your team permission to uphold the same boundary.
- After promoting self-care, schedule a follow-up meeting or conversation with the employee to discuss their progress and any challenges they may be facing. Offer support, reassurance, and additional resources if needed. This demonstrates your ongoing commitment to their well-being and reinforces the importance of self-care within the team culture.

Follow-Up:

After recognizing an employee, follow up. It is crucial to make sure they still feel supported and valued. This prevents them from feeling as if your **CARE** was a show and more about you then it was them. Check in on how they're doing, help them out if they need it, and take action to re-instill the fact you still value them.

Try this:

- After praising an employee's effort, check in on future goals. Let them know it is okay if the next challenge is overwhelming and they need help, regardless of if they knocked it out of the park last time. Give them permission to need help and provide support if they need it.
- After a promotion is given, set up regular mentorship meetings. Ensure that the individual is still being supported in their new tasks.

By taking these steps, leaders can build a culture of acknowledgment and recognition that boosts employee morale, engagement, and overall job satisfaction.

Chapter 2 - Acknowledgment

PUT IT IN ACTION
EMPLOYEE ACKNOWLEDGMENT WORKSHEET

STEP 1: UNDERSTAND EACH TEAM MEMBER

Goals And Aspirations:

- What are their career goals and aspirations?
- How does acknowledging their contributions align with their professional objectives?

Communication Preferences:

- Does the individual prefer public or private acknowledgment?
- How do they like to receive feedback (e.g., in-person, written, team meeting, etc.)?

STEP 2: IDENTIFY SPECIFIC ACHIEVEMENTS

Key Achievements:

- List the specific accomplishments, contributions, or efforts you have observed from them that deserve acknowledgment.

Why It Matters:

- Take a moment to note how these achievements are significant to the team, department, or organization.

STEP 3: PERSONALIZE THE ACKNOWLEDGMENT

Tailoring The Message:

- Craft a personalized message that highlights their unique qualities and contributions.

Preferred Recognition Style:

- Determine whether they would most value a public recognition event, private conversation, or another form of acknowledgment.

STEP 4: INCORPORATE COMPANY VALUES

Aligning With Values:

- How does their contribution align with the core values and culture of your organization?

Highlighting Values:

- In your acknowledgment, emphasize an instance when they have embodied a specific company value.

STEP 5: FOLLOW-UP AND SUPPORT

Post-Acknowledgment Support:

- What steps will you take to ensure they have ongoing support and encouragement?

Future Growth:

How can you help them continue to develop their skills and achieve personal and professional goals?

STEP 6: EXECUTION

Acknowledge:

- Execute the acknowledgment plan as discussed, ensuring it aligns with their preferences. Create a system of accountability for yourself to maintain the plan until your next check-in, in which the plan is updated.

STEP 7: REFLECTION

Feedback and Improvement:

- Gather feedback from your employee about their experience with acknowledgment.
- Reflect on the effectiveness of your acknowledgment and consider improvements for future recognitions.

Remember that effective employee acknowledgment goes beyond a one-time event. It involves understanding, personalization, and ongoing support. When these things are consistently present, we are able to foster a culture of appreciation that motivates our teams and organizations, making work become a place we want to be, find purpose in, and enjoy investing in.

Chapter 2 - Acknowledgment

"CREATING A CULTURE OF INTEGRITY AND ACCOUNTABILITY NOT ONLY IMPROVES EFFECTIVENESS, IT ALSO GENERATES A RESPECTFUL, ENJOYABLE, AND LIFE-GIVING SETTING IN WHICH WE WORK."

TOM HANSON

Respect

Aretha Franklin's anthem "R-E-S-P-E-C-T" is more than just a song; it's a powerful statement that resonates in people's hearts. We all want to be seen and understood, just like Franklin's iconic lyrics. Respect is a vibrant song, full of rhythm. In the same way, respect is an undercurrent at the center of our relationships with others.

Respect recognizes the worth of each person and creates an atmosphere where acceptance and kindness can grow, thus deepening the connection between two people or parties. In essence, Franklin's lyrics remind us that respect is more than just a word; it's a melody that turns ordinary connections into amazing ones.

My definition of mutual respect was sparked by Martha, a great leader who left a lasting impression on me. In the early stages of my career, I was lucky enough to work for her as an Auto Claim Representative. Full of energy, I jumped into the business world and landed with a guide who embodied the true meaning of Respect. Martha was committed to her job, while also setting a high standard for her team. Even though she was very strong and committed to company growth, what made her stand out was the fact she cared deeply about people. For the second time in my career, I was fortunate to work under a **CARES** leader.

Along with her strong exterior, Martha had a gift to see promise in everyone, even newcomers like me. I was positioned in such a way that I could draw ideas from her, all while she pushed me to reach higher goals. I always believed she saw something valuable in me—which speaks to her character and mindset of respect.

But Martha was not simply gracious with words. Her actions backed it up. When my performance didn't live up to her standards, she talked to me about it directly. But even with such accountability, what stood out was how she gave me feedback.

Her style was what made all the difference.

The conversation wasn't steeped in criticism; instead she developed my potential while affirming that she believed in my skills. Martha's example showed how deeply respect and accountability are linked. Her faith in my abilities pushed me to be responsible. This was not out of fear. Instead, it proved we were both committed to reaching the company's goals.

Through Martha's guidance, I understood that respect wasn't just an idea; it was an intangible force that gave people strength to face tangible obstacles. Her demonstrated development and care became the driving force behind my determination to succeed. In turn, I became more responsible and invested in my work. Martha's leadership taught me that genuine care for others can push both individuals and teams to new heights of success, thus proving that respect is not only a virtue but a hidden force for transformative growth.

Chapter 3 - Respect

To understand leadership essentials, we must explore respect. It's not just a buzzword; it's the foundation of all relationships. Yet, many of us struggle to define it. So, before we determine how to act on it, let's unpack the definition of respect.

WHAT IS RESPECT?

In the **CARES** Framework, the "R" signifies caring enough to hold each person on the team accountable. It emphasizes the importance of creating an environment where accountability is valued and nurtured. Holding regular discussions on progress, pitfalls, and solutions demonstrates a leader's commitment to fostering growth and success within the team. By openly addressing challenges and providing support, leaders not only hold individuals accountable for their actions but also empower them to overcome obstacles and reach their full potential. This approach creates a culture of trust and transparency, where team members feel valued and supported in their efforts to give their best.

But, respect can easily take different forms in the minds of various people. Some see it as an obligation to respect elders, such as grandparents, or those in positions of authority, such as teachers or law enforcement personnel. Others view it as something woven into the fabric of each daily encounters, surfaced through small gestures of kindness and politeness.

Just think of how we show our appreciation for others through actions like tipping our hats. All of these are facets of respect. However, respect is more than just polite behavior.

For example, respect also is revealed in adversity.

We see it shine when someone refuses to accept demeaning behavior and confidently stands up for themselves. Additionally, respect isn't limited to interpersonal relationships. It goes beyond that to include concepts like ideology and political boundaries. Saying the Pledge of Allegiance is a powerful act of respect for shared values and unity. Thus, a respectful action become a significant symbol of support for one's nation.

Moreover, Respect resides in subtleties in the workplace, as I experienced with Martha. She showed me respect through politeness, but it was more than that. It was present every time she kept me accountable. This highlighted the vital connection between accountability and esteem. By diving into these complex aspects, we can best appreciate respect as a driving force that improves interpersonal dynamics, encourages teamwork, and helps usher in a more peaceful, interdependent society.

Knowing this, what does respect mean in the workplace?

1 in every 25 employees reports feeling disrespected, unwelcome, or even inferior. This tells me that at least one member on your team is struggling to give their 100%.

But what does this mean for us as leaders? What are our employees seeking from us? According to research published by Kristie Rogers (Associate Professor at Marquette University), two types of respect are highly valued by employees.[16]

The first is "owed respect," which meets the need for each individual to feel like they belong. It manifests itself via kindness and an environment where people feels like they matter. When owed respect is lacking, it demonstrates itself as actions that harm the workplace, such as excessive monitoring and micromanagement, rudeness, and the abuse of power.

"Earned respect," however, rewards employees who exhibit qualities or behaviors which align with company values. An emphasis on earned respect creates a way to recognize employees who go above and above, while also validating the fact that every

Chapter 3 - Respect

employee, particularly those in knowledge-based fields, also possess unique abilities. Thus, this form of respect is fostered because of good work accomplished.

Respectful behavior looks like:

- Demonstrating politeness and courtesy
- Actively engaging in conversations
- Embracing diverse perspectives
- Fostering open communication
- Avoiding gossip
- Expressing appreciation
- Ensuring each individual feels included
- Using clear and understandable language
- Offering sincere apologies when necessary

When it comes to leadership, respect reaches past the superficial theory of mutual acknowledgment. Mutual acknowledgment is good. It is a desirable quality. But it is only a base courtesy. Instead, respect is something we carry in the core of who we are. It comes from a place in which we care about each person on the team enough to hold them accountable. It's an attitude we create which lends to an atmosphere of trust and openness. It gives space for consistent check-ins about progress and problems. It reaches beyond tick-box performance reviews and dives into to the heart of what employees want and the challenges they face.

Leaders who lead their teams with respect know that accountability isn't about micromanagement or hierarchies. Instead, it's about developing each person in a way which allows them to see their own potential all while providing the tools they need to use that potential to make an invested contribution to the organization's goals. This level of respect requires leaders to provide each person on their team with genuine understanding, empathy, and a commitment to fostering an environment where that single team member can thrive.

RESPECT IS NOT

We have looked at what respect is. But let's also dive into what it is not in order to fully understand its depths.

Some may define respect as if it was a mark of authority which acts as a blank check for bullying, harassment, or coercion. But such a limiting, title-only emphasis misses the beauty of genuine respect.

Respect doesn't mean ignoring someone's thoughts, feelings, or contributions. It also doesn't mean ignoring their presence or lowering their worth. When it comes to equality and inclusion, Respect doesn't mean treating people differently because of their race, gender, age, religion, or sexual orientation. It also doesn't mean devaluing one group to value the other.

No matter which emphasis you are highlighting, respect never needs to demean in order to showcase. It doesn't stand for intolerant points of view. Instead, it means supporting open communication and understanding, even when people disagree.

Respect does not stoop to use insulting language, make threats, or hurt someone physically or mentally. It will never cross personal lines or invade privacy because it knows how important privacy, permission, and personal space are.

Respect recognizes the error of believing we are better than someone else. Instead, it avoids condescension, attitude, or a sense of entitlement. True respect is given to everyone, no matter what they've done or how well they are known in society.

In this sense, it is akin to dignity. And I think you and I would both agree that the world would be a better place with more dignity in it.

Chapter 3 - Respect

We can cultivate that dignity by forming a respectful workplace for our teams. We want them to walk away feeling as if:

- They've been treated with respect and appreciation, and it shows.
- It's okay to be different.
- They have been treated as they want to be treated
- It is okay to talk about problems and try to find answers.
- They are aware that action will be taken quickly when inappropriate or disrespectful conduct occurs.

WHY IS RESPECT IMPORTANT?

Respect isn't just a nice thing to do; it's a transformative force that can change the core of how organizations work. Mental health is significantly boosted when respect is present. When **CARES** leadership is present in the workplace, employees feel seen, appreciated, heard, and helped. This emotional safety net lowers stress and anxiety, making it possible for people to excel.

We all face incredible challenges. While the reason we were hired is to meet the expectations of our companies, we also are up against personal obstacles including crisis. And organizations who understand this—instead of scoff at it—earn their employees loyalty. Imagine what would happen if the next time a team member is not at their peak performance due to personal problem, they were cared for instead of criticized. What would happen if their coworkers showed kindness and understanding, and withheld judgment—even if it meant they had to take extra time to support him or her. This act of care not only helps the struggling employee's mental health, but it also makes the team stronger, creating an environment of trust and kindness.

Respect also acts as a mirror for responsibility. People are more likely to take responsibility for their actions when they feel respected. Imagine a mistake is made as a result of poor communication. How do you think that will play out in an environment which has fostered respect?

I have seen it firsthand. When people work in a respectful setting, they are encouraged to own up to their mistakes, learn from them, and create solutions. This level of accountability not only resolves the problem quickly, but also builds a mindset of responsibility. In turn, it makes the workplace better because honesty is valued.

Respect also accepts differences, versus merely tolerating them. In such a workplace, people with different backgrounds, points of view, and experiences are not only accepted, but they are also celebrated for what they bring to the table. Creative problem-solving thrives when workers from different perspectives are asked for their insight and ideas. This variety leads to creativity and makes the workplace lively and active.

Respect also binds individuals together. Colleagues work in lock step when they esteem each other's ideas and contributions. Imagine a concepting session where each idea is valued. Though not every one of them will be acted on, airing them establishes respect that promotes belonging and worth. As feedback is provided, it also refines and sharpens each individual in the room. As decisions are made collectively, each person feels excitement and ownership of the project. Such Respect makes work more congruent and leads to better relationships between team members.

Additionally, respect is key to fixing problems and ending arguments. When we treat each other with respect, we are more likely to be open and have honest conversations. Have you ever seen the opposite in effect?

Chapter 3 - Respect

I bet you have known two people on the same team who didn't agree with each other. But have you ever seen that same scenario when they were able to talk about their problems without fear in a safe place? It fosters solutions that work for everyone. This method of solving a problem, rooted in mutual respect, makes it easier for everyone to reach goals together in the future.

Respect makes us more engaged and productive. At work, when people are treated with respect, they feel like their efforts are valued and recognized. This confirmation fuels their drive, which up-levels productivity.

For example, if a leader was to praise an employee's creative thinking, that comment would not only boost confidence but also motivate them to do their best work. In turn, this increases the organization's output.

Did you know that respect is also a great way to relieve stress? A workplace culture where people accept each other's boundaries greatly lowers stress. Take the example of an employee with too much on his plate. If his team were to value his time and provide help, this would lower his worry. Therefore, knowing where each other are at and respecting it in a way which doesn't take over but supports, builds community. This establishes an environment where people can do their best work without headaches, racing hearts, and sweaty palms over looming deadlines.

Lastly, respect establishes culture which is rooted in fairness and equality. When respect guides a decision-making process, employees perceive the company to be fair and just. One way to promote this is to ensure that promotions are based on skills and merit. This shows that you value each worker's skill-set versus playing favorites. It creates a workplace where everyone has an equal chance to succeed.

In the end, when defining respect we must recognize that it isn't just an idea; it's a powerful force that makes organizations successful. Its benefits are vast: mental health is valued, responsibility is upheld, diversity is embraced, relationships are strengthened, problem-solving is improved, productivity soars, stress levels drop, and fairness rules.

By forging a culture of respect, companies give their workers power, while also setting the stage for a successful, peaceful, and creative workplace where diverse individuals have room to thrive.

THE FIRST STEP

Let's take it back to Aretha Franklin's lyrics from "R-E'S-P-E-C-T." These powerful words invoke a sense of confidence and dedication for listeners. In the same way, leaders must create an environment of mutual respect in a business, thus compelling team members to follow the example. But you may be asking, "Where do I begin?"

For me, Martha set my life on a trajectory of constantly wanting to both earn and provide respect to others. I know the benefit of watching what great leaders do and how they make decisions. Because of this, I can confidently say that respect is not just an idea; it's a real force that shapes the way every company works.

As leaders, we carry the torch and set the tone for everyone within the workplace. This beckons me to make sure that everyone on the team feels valued and respected by encouraging empathy, active listening, and understanding. I want to provide a feeling of justice and belonging by accepting others as they are, valuing differences, and treating everyone the same.

We have the privilege of making respect become more than ideology and transform it into tangible, actionable practices. In turn,

Chapter 3 - Respect

this makes respect a daily habit woven into our organization's core. Like Aretha's unshakable confidence in her song, I know we have power to show respect, making the workplace a space in which mutual respect is an expected standard.

Implementing the following principles and strategies are just a handful of ways to foster a culture of mutual respect within your organization:

Recognition

- Every background, experience, and point of view is valued and publicly recognized in a workplace that values diversity. Imagine working in a place where people from various demographics are not only welcomed, but also valued. Such openness creates a strong sense of belonging, reducing loneliness and improving mental health.

Try this:

- Implement a structured recognition program where employees' diverse backgrounds and achievements are celebrated publicly. Use several platforms including team meetings, newsletters, and/or internal communication channels to acknowledge and appreciate unique contributions.

Encourage

- In a respectful workplace, everyone's work is noticed and appreciated, no matter their job or title. When praise is offered at every level, it raises morale, which builds pride.

Try this:

- Encourage coworkers to openly praise each other's work and create an atmosphere of peer-to-peer recognition. Set up a "kudos board" or an online compliment portal for employees to praise their coworkers' work. This fosters an environment where people feel seen and supported.

Support

- Collaboration and good communication are the fuel which keep Respect alive in the workplace. A friendly environment is the natural result of open communication and working together. Supportive team meetings mean everyone's voice is heard and valued. Every department gets a voice. Every team member feels like a contributor.

Try this:

- Team-building events, workshops, and brainstorming sessions are just a few avenues which break up familiar routines and help people to work together. Prioritize and publicly praise when you see open communication and discussions in which everyone's opinion is valued. Boost your workers sense of support by offering skill development and mentorship programs.

Promote Fairness

- Equal treatment sits at the heart of respect. Fair treatment equates to safety. Both ensure that everyone feels appreciated at work.

Chapter 3 - Respect

Try this:

- Establish clear paths for raises and awards to be given. Promote based on quantitative facts such as skills, accomplishments, and credentials. Regularly communicate the criteria and processes for advancement. This will help the company to be seen as fair and as if everyone is afforded the same chance to accelerate.

Empathy

- Listening with empathy is a characteristic of Respect. When workers feel heard, they feel supported as they face problems and take on new experiences. Imagine what it is like to have a manager who leans in and listens to concerns, ideas, and even frustration. Such recognition boosts confidence and mental toughness, giving people confidence.

Try this:

- Hold an active listening workshop or empathy training sessions. Encourage managers to meet with employees one-on-one and practice listening, focusing on demonstrating that they care. Giving managers tools to develop their own emotional intelligence creates an environment of support and understanding.

Cultivate Understanding

- Sincere explanations matter, especially when one's words or actions unintentionally hurt someone. We all know how much easier it is for us to understand and accept an apology when someone admits their mistakes and show that they are sorry. Such humility and ownership can allow the other to heal emotionally while also championing for feedback on how to avoid future mistakes.

Try this:

- Empower your employees by hosting inclusion trainings which highlight different cultures, beliefs, and points of view. Give your employees a safe place to ask questions about cultural differences and share their stories. This promotes understanding and builds awareness with each other. Always encourage leaders to own their mistakes, apologize, and seek to learn from each encounter.

Transparency

- Clear conversations, regular feedback, and a fair distribution of work are all important qualities. When employees are well-informed, receive helpful feedback, and are given appropriate workloads, stress and uncertainty diminish.

Try this:

- Establish a process for employees to give you feedback on your leadership. This can happen in one-to-one settings or by using anonymous forums. Additionally, make sure that changes, goals, and challenges facing the company are communicated upfront. Set clear rules for planning work ensuring employees aren't overworked and stress levels are reduced. Share comments quickly and on time. This helps employees grow professionally and mentally because the feedback was linked to something in the present.

These principles of Respect, when used in tandem with your company's values, have power to create a workplace where workers feel respected, supported, and own the organization's mission.

Chapter 3 - Respect

PUT IT IN ACTION
EMPLOYEE RESPECT WORKSHEET

STEP 1: IMPLEMENT A STRUCTURED RECOGNITION PROGRAM

Create A Recognition Calendar:

Schedule regular events to publicly appreciate employees' diverse backgrounds and accomplishments. Encourage team members to nominate their peers for recognition, creating a positive atmosphere of acknowledgment and celebration.

Reflection Questions:

- What unique qualities or achievements can I recognize in my team members?
- How can I encourage employees to nominate their peers for recognition?
- How can I tailor recognition events to individual preferences?

STEP 2: FOSTER PEER-TO-PEER RECOGNITION

Establish A "Kudos Board" Or Online Platform:

Set up a digital space where employees can praise their coworkers openly for their hard work. Encourage team members to share specific examples of their peer's positive impact. Reward active participation to enhance motivation.

Reflection Questions:

- How can I create a culture where employees freely acknowledge other's achievements?
- What incentives can I introduce which will encourage active participation on the recognition platform?
- How can I ensure recognition is sincere and meaningful among team members?

STEP 3: FACILITATE TEAM COLLABORATION AND OPEN COMMUNICATION

Organize Team-Building Workshops:

Conduct team-building events, workshops, or brainstorming sessions to enhance collaboration. Ensure open communication and active participation, valuing everyone's input. Provide skill development and mentorship programs to foster support and connection.

Reflection Questions:

- What team-building activities align with our goals and encourage collaboration?
- How can I facilitate open communication during workshops, ensuring everyone's voice is heard?
- What mentorship programs would benefit specific team members, and how can I initiate them?

STEP 4: ENSURE TRANSPARENT PROCESSES

Conduct Promotion Criteria Workshop:

Explain promotion criteria and processes clearly. Address questions and concerns, providing examples of how both skills and achievements are evaluated. Foster understanding and confidence in the fairness of the promotion process.

Reflection Questions:

- What common misconceptions about promotion criteria may need clarification?
- How can I proactively address employees' questions about the promotion process?
- What steps can be added to ensure transparency in decision-making?

STEP 5: ENHANCE LISTENING SKILLS AND EMOTIONAL INTELLIGENCE

Host Active Listening Workshops:

Organize active listening workshops or empathy training sessions for managers and employees. Encourage managers to hold one-on-one sessions allowing them to actively listen to employee concerns, while demonstrating empathy and support. Provide tools to enhance emotional intelligence, creating a supportive and understanding environment.

Reflection Questions:

- How can I encourage employees to share their concerns openly during one-on-one sessions?
- What active listening workshops are available?
- How can I promote a culture where empathy and understanding are valued?
- How can I model empathy to my managers who I expect to provide it for their team?

STEP 6: PROMOTE CULTURAL AWARENESS AND INCLUSION

Conduct Diversity And Inclusion Training Programs:

Implement trainings which inform employees about different cultures, beliefs, and perspectives. Create a safe space for employees to discuss cultural differences and share experiences. Encourage leaders to admit mistakes, apologize sincerely, and demonstrate a willingness to learn from them, fostering an inclusive workplace.

Reflection Questions:

- How can I facilitate open discussions about cultural differences?
- What strategies can I implement to ensure leaders actively participate in diversity and inclusion training?
- How can I quantify understanding and acceptance?

STEP 7: ESTABLISH CLEAR COMMUNICATION CHANNELS

Implement Feedback Mechanisms:

Set up regular employee-to-manager feedback for employees to share their concerns. Consider using methods such as quarterly performance reviews on the leader or anonymous suggestion boxes. Ensure employees can express their thoughts openly. Communicate changes, goals, and challenges clearly. Define workload planning rules to prevent overworking, keeping stress levels low. Encourage managers to provide timely comments, fostering professional and mental growth.

Chapter 3 - Respect

Reflection Questions:

- How can I create a safe environment for my employees to share honest feedback about my management?
- What steps can I take to ensure transparent communication regarding organizational changes and challenges?
- How can I support managers by providing timely, constructive feedback that promotes growth?

Remember:

Taking action and reflecting on impact enables leaders to create an environment where Respect is not an idea alone—but it is a fundamental part of the organization's culture. When acted on, these steps build a workplace where employees feel valued, supported, and connected. This ripple effect moves outward and creates enhanced teamwork, productivity, and overall well-being.

Chapter 3 - Respect

"YOUR TIME IS LIMITED, SO DON'T WASTE IT LIVING SOMEONE ELSE'S LIFE. DON'T BE TRAPPED BY DOGMA—WHICH IS LIVING WITH THE RESULTS OF OTHER PEOPLE'S THINKING. DON'T LET THE NOISE OF OTHERS' OPINIONS DROWN OUT YOUR OWN INNER VOICE. AND, MOST IMPORTANT, HAVE THE COURAGE TO FOLLOW YOUR HEART AND INTUITION..."

STEVE JOBS

Empower 4

Have you ever had a leader who gave you freedom to be your authentic self? Have you experienced an environment where conformity wasn't the name of the game? I am fortunate to say that I have. I will be forever grateful to Tom, my Team Manager, who became a game-changer in how I defined leadership.

Tom wasn't just successful as a manger and employee; he embodied the meaning of what success could look like—what it meant to meet deadlines, all while still having fun and demonstrating care. Imagine that! His leadership wasn't consumed by seriousness. Instead, he savored opportunities for each of his team members. He encouraged us to be ourselves and we enjoyed the journey towards success together.

If I had to identify the key element which made Tom a standout leader—I would have to highlight his knack for genuine connection. With Tom, morning check-ins weren't a data-dump in which he sought updates on the project. Instead, he connected with you as a person. This didn't mean that the work didn't matter. It did. Inevitably, we would end up discussing those components as well, but he didn't come in guns a blazing.

His first priority was for you as a person. Each morning, he'd inquire about our well-being and family. To me, working on this team was like joining an extended family, and Tom was at the helm.

Looking back at my time under his leadership, I can pinpoint the fact that he had an uncanny ability to sense if you were having an off day—all without prying. And the best part? His door was always open, ready for a chat whenever you needed it. I never felt like I interrupted him, made his workday worse with my issue, or that I was in his way.

Even when I started at the organization and I felt like a puzzle piece struggling to find its place, Tom made me feel like I belonged. It was as if he lived the mantra: *No judgment here.*

He exuded authenticity, creating an environment where you felt empowered to be yourself, no apologies necessary. He didn't care about hair style, wardrobe specifics, or the size of your hoop earrings. And while those might seem like small things, they lay a foundation for bigger ones. That type of openness for self-expression in the small made me feel like I had the ability to express myself in other areas, to the point that I began to trust the fact that my voice mattered when it came to working under his direction. I resonated with the space he provided for authenticity. Tom knew that belonging and authenticity were the secret sauce of leadership. His recipe it worked like magic throughout the organization.

I love to talk about Tom, and the impact he made on my professional development, because his level of care for each of his team members personified the definition of empowerment.

Empowerment, within the **CARES** Model, means showing that we genuinely care for everyone within our team, granting them the

Chapter 4 - Empower

freedom to be authentic and embrace their uniqueness without any pressure to conform.

When a leader adopts this mindset of empowerment, their employees are seen as more than just contributors to a deadline or goal. Instead, they're valued individuals who perceive that they belong. They are secure and know that they do not have to mold themselves to fit a predetermined "one-size-fits-all," standard-issue employee model.

The E in our **CARES** Model is a reminder to empower each of our team members by fostering an environment where authenticity goes beyond personal satisfaction. It is also a powerful leadership tool that propels individuals to unlock their full potential.

For when people are empowered to be authentic, they become the architects of their success.

AUTHENTICITY DEFINED

"Authenticity" is a concept which is deeper than just knowing what it means to be honest with yourself. It goes beyond the mantra that we must "be ourselves." It is about resonating with your identity to such a degree that there is a full embodiment of it, in every environment, without shame or insecurity.

This is quite a challenge to achieve, but we must unlock such power within ourselves. The challenge? How do we reach such a state? While messages which tell us to "be ourselves" are good, more opportunity is needed. After all, it is hard to find useful advice on *how* to be authentic.

Instead, what individuals crave are for coaches and leaders to draw this authenticity out of them, empowering them to be the best version of themselves, all without diminishing them in the process to achieving it. Thus, insightful and caring leaders in the workplace can serve as a catalyst for deep development.

Being authentic begins with self-awareness. This means it is our responsibility to understand our values, emotions, and skills, as well as how other people see us. Such insight grants us the ability to know what to tell them and when.

To be self-aware requires a deep study of oneself and the world around us—and it reaps rewards as we begin to know how to navigate what it means to be authentic in a complicated world. Our journey begins as we learn to think deeply about who we are and how the world affects us.

TO BE OR NOT TO BE AUTHENTIC

Achieving authenticity within the workplace is not an easy task. It requires a great deal of personal introspection and care—no matter if you are a leader or team member. Regardless of role, defining our true self at work is like a delicate dance of complicated dynamics, social expectations, and various levels of vulnerability required as we determine where it is appropriate to be open about who we really are.

Authenticity is not like flipping a switch. Achieving self-awareness is something which requires dedication. It is a complex process of self-discovery and taking care of oneself, often labeled as "Inner Work®." But how important that work is!

Though it is not tangible, doing the inner work occurs when we reflect on our values, beliefs, and goals. In doing so, we will brush up against any social norms or work structures that challenge our authenticity.

Chapter 4 - Empower

Concealing one's authentic self at work was a necessity once seen as important to modern workplace culture. But this trend is fading. Early adopters who have empowered their team members to express their authentic identity and create a culture of belonging have organizations which are reported to be positive and welcoming. The result has been an increase in engagement and productivity.

But even in a supportive, empowered culture, we still must consider the additional challenges that people from disadvantaged groups face. Not everyone has the same opportunities. Even positive empowerment movements must take into account the variety of backgrounds and biases that affect each individual's work experience.

The pressure to fit in is a phenomenon most employees struggle with at one time or another—especially in seasons of transition. But this is heightened for workers whose culture or identity is not well-represented. This leads to a fear of being misread, left out, or even punished for certain parts of one's being. As a result, some workers will choose to hide parts of who they are—even when that part of them is crucial to their sense of self.

Survival plays out—causing concealment—which causes inner distress. The ripple effect of such a course of action is an inner war. Instead of work being a safe place to be yourself, it becomes a breeding ground for anxiety in which you must find a careful balance between fitting in and being yourself.

Most of us have felt the weight of this tension at one point or another. And yet, for some—this is the everyday norm. The fear of being judged, the need to fit in with social rules, and the possibility of facing consequences at work fight against us many as they seek to be authentic.

As a black woman, I remember my own struggle in this complicated area. Simply determining how to style my hair is one such example. My hair is naturally curly, yet I had been conditioned to believe that I had to style it in a certain way to be perceived as professional. Because I feared being judged and valued fitting in, I chose straight, permed hair. Additionally, I never wore any of my large hoop earrings which I wore in every environment other than work. This was the price I felt I had to pay in order to fit into a corporate mold.

I put on a disingenuous front of "corporate me" for years. I frequently felt fear of judgment and carried internal anxiety to not stand out, even at the expense of the ways I naturally expressed myself.

Thus, I carried the weight of constantly calculating if I fit in or not during each workday, in every meeting, and in each conversation with my leadership. Then I met Tom.

The freedom he provided for our team helped me to understand that being authentic wasn't simply a line item on a benefit plan. It wasn't something "nice-to-have." Instead, it was a personal must.

Being empowered to be my authentic self was necessary if I was going to find both personal and work happiness. I didn't even realize I had been burned out; but I finally recognized the fact that I hadn't been authentic for most of my career before that point. With a new environment under Tom's leadership, I saw that my true self was different from the character I created in order to fit social norms.

This change took time. Through self-reflection, I started to question the accepted norms I had adopted. I began small and began to pivot slowly. This was as much a moment of courage for me as it was a social experiment on how others received my changes. But with time, I began to have small personal victories as I embraced who I was.

I began to have pride for my natural curls and discarded the perms. I felt a new sense of personal dignity as I began to see how uniquely different I was. I saw it as a positive thing to express my creativity in how I styled my hair and what accessories I chose. I kept my look clean, well-groomed, and professional while still making it a point to showcase my genuine, fun-loving personality.

In turn, I began to feel care-free in my interactions with others. My inter-office exchanges became relaxed as I began to embrace an abundance of fun and laughter with my peers. I felt powerful when I relinquished fake layers of conformity. I found courage to portray an authentic mindset which exuded: "I am going to be who I am."

WHAT MAKES PEOPLE CONFORM

The desire to fit in is highly nuanced. Yet, it is worth unpacking since this unspoken weight is present in our complicated world of workplace dynamics. We must look at the unconscious biases present which shape individuals' need to conform.

Patricia Hewlin delved into the established rules and organizational ideals that compel employees to conform. Her work reveals a mix of conscious and unconscious behaviors. She recognizes the fact that individuals may unknowingly align with prevailing norms in order to feel a sense of belonging.[17] Therefore, as leaders, it is our job to be aware of these constructs at play in our offices—and empower authenticity within our people.

Biases which affect employees include:

Affinity Bias:

This phenomenon occurs as people naturally draw toward people who are like them. As a result, this can form exclusive groups. This leads people outside the majority to feel pushed to the edges, making it harder for them to be authentic.

Stereotype Danger:

Preconceived ideas regarding people groups force those individuals to conform to societal expectations, thus limiting their authenticity. At times, this means over-performing to prove they do not fit the norm. Other times, it means avoiding certain situations in order to skirt the preconceived notion. Pressure to fit in and avoid these ideas stops people from expressing themselves honestly. As a result, they portray a version of themselves that fits what they believe others want to see.

Microaggressions:

Rude or hurtful microaggressions can crush the spirit. Even situations which are unintentional can leave people feeling uncomfortable and as if they must avoid being themselves in order to avoid future microaggressions. These actions, especially when directed towards people from underrepresented groups, make the workplace feel unwelcoming or hostile. This only serves to increase the challenges of those seeking to be themselves, without knowing how—or *if* it is even safe.

When employees hide their opinions and echo the stance that the majority of people in the company support—you can be sure that biases are present. It is actually healthy to have a variety of opinions. This may come as a shock for most leaders.

Yet, having diverse input within your organization helps to create services or products which meet the needs of a diverse customer base. Thus, a healthy exchange of different views is crucial. And it is our job, as leaders, to foster them.

Chapter 4 - Empower

So how do we identify the ways in which our people may feel pressure to confirm? The complicated factors that affect how people act at work are not easy to identify. But we must do the hard work of identifying areas of false conformity so we can empower our people to be authentic from within.

Types of conformity which are common include:

Uniformity In Communication Styles:

Employees often adopt a communication style that matches the company's tone, even if it's not their natural style.

Dress Code Compliance:

Employees may repress their personal style to fit the company's professional image.

Consensus-Driven Decision-Making:

Employees who avoid discussing an opposing view during a group discussion may be conforming to the majority.

Adopting Common Work Habits:

Even if common work habits like start and end hours, break schedules, and task execution methods do not fit the employee's personal productivity patterns, they may conform to expectations, thus limiting their best output.

Conformity With Organizational Values:

Even if their personal opinions differ, employees may express personal alignment with organizational values for the sake of fitting into company culture.

Consistent Social Behavior:

Employees may conform by attending particular social activities, following certain manners, or accommodating social hierarchy—at the expense of self.

Echoing Leadership Styles:

To appear compatible with leadership, employees may mimic a superior's communication, decision-making, and problem-solving styles.

Mirroring Team Dynamics:

Employees may mirror their behavior and contributions to resemble a dominant team member or vocal leader, sometimes at the price of their particular abilities.

Conformity damages authenticity. While it may be believed that shutting down one's natural style is important for keeping a group together, it does more damage by shutting down unique voices and points of view.

Pressure to belong stops honest expression, which stalls the growth of an open and creative workplace. Recognizing and dealing with these conformist habits is not only important for leaders to remove barriers of authenticity, but it is also crucial for empowering employees to be more involved in their work. Providing freedom to belong reaps great rewards, not only personally but professionally—as authentic workplaces create environments where each employee can thrive.

Chapter 4 - Empower

THE BENEFITS OF AUTHENTICITY

Authenticity is more than a personal virtue. When done right, it benefits the overall performance of a company.

The Institute for Inclusive Leadership conducted a study on authenticity in the workplace. They found that people who reported freedom to be themselves at work are happier with their jobs. 71% are more sure of themselves, 60% are more interested, and 46% are happy. More than one-third of those who contributed to the study stated that being authentic made them happier not only at work, but also in their personal life.[18]

Survey respondents who reported freedom to be authentic at work also shared the impact of that freedom. Their responses included:

- I am more committed to staying with my organization (30%)
- I am more able to do my best work (52%)
- I build stronger relationships with my colleagues (53%)
- I am more effective (48%)
- I am more productive (44%)
- I am more likely to go "above and beyond" for my organization (42%)[19]

Such results prove that authenticity effects the individual and organization's well-being. In addition to quantitative measures of workplace happiness, the qualitative measures of personal fulfillment and contentment show the value of empowerment.

When employees can be themselves at work, they see their personal and business lives fit holistically. This combination creates a complete sense of self with a state of well-being that extends beyond the workplace and makes the person behind the employee stronger and happier.

And yet, the benefits go even further. Inter-personal relationships within the workplace are also positively affected. Respondents reported an increase in the quality of relationships they had with coworkers when they felt free to be themselves. Their ability to connect socially was foundational for them to experience teamwork, creativity, and a sense of belonging within their organization. Thus, being authentic isn't something one person has or doesn't have. Instead, it effects the quality of relationship between workers—something which is foundational to any successful team.

When workers are empowered to be authentic, the business benefits. Respondents demonstrate the fact that personal happiness and the success of the organization go hand-in-hand. Individuals who genuinely enjoy their job show a strong dedication to their companies. They also desire to remain loyal contributors.

Together, this commitment matched with higher effectiveness and productivity make the company stronger and better at what it does. Empowered employees who feel seen, heard, and understood are ready to go "above and beyond" for their companies. This proves that authenticity is a catalyst for change and springboard to create a culture of dedication and innovation. Over time, authenticity moves from a personal choice into being a strategic necessity for creating a culture that values happiness, commitment, collaboration, and long-term success.

For authenticity to become a driving force within your organization, consider these various dimensions:

Stronger Team Dynamic:

- Being authentic builds a strong team dynamic. People who are honest create an environment where trust grows. When people on a team feel free to be themselves, they have room to understand and accept each other. This trust fosters

smooth conversation and the growth of strong working relationships. When people on a team are encouraged to be themselves, they are more likely to share different points of view and new ideas without fear of being judged.
This creates a setting in which each person is given opportunities to learn and grow from others who are different from them.

Fuel Innovation:

- Empowerment provides space for individuals to share different points of view without fear of being judged. When people are authentic, they feel free to think outside the box, share their ideas, and question the status quo. These different points of view spark new ideas and innovative answers.

Better Customer Experiences:

- Authenticity shapes connections with customers as well as interactions within a company. People who are more authentic tend to connect with clients on a deeper level. Thus, being given freedom of expression they often "pay-it-forward" and seek to understand customer/client wants and concerns. This threshold of honesty forges long-lasting relationships with customers, boosting trust and loyalty to the brand. Honesty is bedrock to a positive business image and bolsters a sense of credibility with the market and individual customers.

Improved Employee Engagement:

- Leaders and team members who are honest motivate their peers to adopt honesty. Authenticity creates a workplace in which people feel seen and appreciated for the unique skills and talents they bring to the table. Specialized and unique praise grants people a sense of purpose and belonging. The result? Once more, this drives employees to go above and beyond in their jobs, boosting productivity.

Keeping Good Employees:

- Companies who value sincerity tend to keep their best employees. When people feel valued, they are less inclined to seek esteem elsewhere. When an organization's culture supports authenticity, it retains professionals who thrive within honest self-expression.

A LEADER'S ROLE IN AUTHENTICITY

The unique qualities inside each employee make the workplace vivacious. Every team member is part of shaping company culture since the environment is shaped by how each person sees themselves and others. Leaders who seek to create an authentic workplace must leverage this in a way which promotes dignity and diversity. Our goal is to build a place that everyone in the company can relate to.

It's not enough to make statements which honor diversity. To see this value come to life you must work to make sure every employee feels seen, heard, and free to express themselves. This means actively supporting a genuine exchange of ideas. Leaders are catalysts who bring about this cultural shift. They are crucial to steering the company toward a place where authenticity isn't more than a buzzword. They are the ones who make it a deeply ingrained and celebrated part of their workplace.

Chapter 4 - Empower

THE CHALLENGES

Establishing an atmosphere of authenticity is not easy. Numerous problems arise when initiating it. Traditional hierarchical systems, which serve as barriers for speaking freely, are tremendous issues. A top-down approach often instills fear in workers which leave them to feel judged or punished if their role is not perceived as significant. Leaders must break down these barriers from the top. We have the ability and responsibility to create an atmosphere where everyone on the team feels free to share their thoughts and ideas honestly.

Next, we are able to tackle deeply ingrained rules that value conformity over authenticity in our interactions, teams, and departments. Uniformity hinders unique thoughts and views. To break these rules, leaders must question the status quo and encourage people to remain open to different points of view. This will result in pushing workers to be themselves, even if that is different from how they have presented themselves in the past.

Hidden biases can be found in every corner in the workplace. But leaders are positioned to challenge harmful mindsets within their own sphere of influence. To do so, actions steps include training our teams, raising awareness of biases, and actively working to stop discriminating behaviors.

By standing up for belonging, leaders combat their own fear of being open and vulnerable. Leaders are typically perceived as strong and stubborn. Therefore, it can be hard for them to show their own vulnerabilities, including misunderstandings or biases. But being open to reveal their own hurts or mistakes is an integral part of authenticity. Leaders who demonstrate that being open isn't a sign of weakness *but a strength* are able to help their team to trust and connect with each other.

They have proved that it is safe to do, and leave a path to follow.

Lastly, leaders may have the best intentions when it comes to cultivating authenticity—yet may find their biggest challenge to be finding time to develop an authentic culture. Deadlines, reaching goals, and current issues all tend to compete with initiatives for authenticity. Leaders who are striving for empowerment will be required to find their own balance. But for those who are daring to make such incredible strides, I want you to know that I see you and I am proud of the investment of time, focus, and energy that you are giving to your team. Your organization is a stronger place for what you are dedicating to empowerment.

Together, we are creating spaces where the authentic is not only welcomed, but an important part of culture.

A LEADER'S PATH TO CREATING A CULTURE OF AUTHENTICITY

Leaders who seek to create an authentic workplace culture must act on five strategic steps, including:

Step 1. Lead Authentically:

- Demonstrate authenticity by revealing your own struggles, wins, and failures. Being open and vulnerable sets the tone that openness is a value you are willing to model and provide room for.

Step 2. Define Core Values:

- Clearly state and communicate the organization's values. These must stress sincerity, diversity, and inclusion. Make sure that everyone in the company brings these values into their tasks and decision-making moments.

Chapter 4 - Empower

Step 3. Encourage Inclusion:

- Actively create an inclusive atmosphere by ensuring that everyone on the team feels valued and heard. To foster transparency, encourage different points of view and set up numerous lines of contact for honest exchange.

Step 4. Deal With Unconscious Biases:

- Utilize trainings in which to teach your employees how to spot and question unconscious biases. Forming common language and processes around eliminating conformity make the workplace universally open and honest.

Step 5. Recognize And Reward Authenticity:

- Recognize and reward actions which were made from a place of authenticity. Encourage those who demonstrate belonging amidst their peers. Leaders show that authenticity is valued when they recognize and appreciate it.

Creating an empowered, authentic environment in your team is a transformational process. It will not come easily, and it takes intentionality.

To be successful, you will be required to actively challenge deeply rooted norms. This will not always be comfortable for you as a leader. But it is worth it to cultivate a place where people feel free to be themselves.

Myths about authenticity can be eradicated when leaders practice vulnerability, open communication, and demonstrate a dedication to improvement. By doing this, they not only create a culture of belonging, but they also empower the company to reach long-term success, to spark new ideas, and to forge a sense of community.

Chapter 4 - Empower

PUT IT IN ACTION
EMPLOYEE EMPOWERMENT WORKSHEET

STEP 1: ASK YOURSELF WHAT AUTHENTIC LEADERSHIP MEANS TO YOU.

Start by thinking about your leadership style and how it aligns with authenticity.

Ask Yourself:

- In terms of being real, how are you currently setting a good example?
- What action can you take to show that you are open and vulnerable?
- How often do you speak about or promote the organization's core values?

STEP 2: WRITE DOWN AND TALK ABOUT YOUR CORE VALUES.

Review and define your organization's core ideals as a team. Facilitate points of conversation which stress authenticity, diversity, and acceptance. Prompt everyone on the team to share their ideas and thoughts.

Ask Yourself:

- What ideas do you believe the team is most aligned in?
- How can each value be championed for in a way which empowers team members to make decisions?

STEP 3: PRACTICE INCLUSION

Practice making the team environment welcoming to everyone. Facilitate discussions and events which allow team members to share ideas and experiences. Include topics such as fear of repercussion regarding honesty in the workplace.

Ask Yourself:

- What problems might my team be facing when it comes to inclusivity?
- How can my team work to make our workplace more welcoming?

STEP 4: TRAINING TO GET RID OF UNCONSCIOUS BIAS.

Set up a workshop to understand unconscious bias. This could be led externally or internally. Discuss how biases affect sincerity and create ways to increase belonging while diminishing biases in your organization. Create scheduled check -ins to follow up on the plan you created together using several calendar benchmarks.

Ask Yourself:

- How can my team identify and eliminate hidden biases?
- What programs can I utilize to increase understanding and reduce bias?

STEP 5: APPRECIATION OF AUTHENTIC CONTRIBUTIONS

Establish methods for your team to recognize belonging and inclusive efforts and then reward it. Create meaningful ways to recognize authenticity, which will reinforce its worth in the company's culture.

Chapter 4 - Empower

Ask Yourself:

- How can I recognize and praise genuine efforts?
- What forms of recognition would motivate my team to be authentic?

PLAN OF ACTION

This week, process what you learned from the above worksheet tasks. Write down your observations and create a personal plan of action to initiate this quarter. Outline your specific steps and due dates to put these strategies in place, thus forming an empowered, authentic culture in your workplace.

Ask Yourself:

- What immediate steps can I take to encourage authenticity?
- What metrics can I use to keep track of and measure progress over time?

Remember:

This leadership development worksheet is meant to establish practical next steps. You do not have to do this alone. Cultivating your empowered culture of authenticity alongside your team members is key to building an environment that allows people to thrive. Your pledge to pursue authenticity will remain intact as long as you champion for it and allow your action plan to be reviewed and renewed on a regular basis.

The investment is steep. And yet, the dividends reap rich rewards both for you as a leader—and for each person in your realm of influence.

Chapter 4 - Empower

"A LEADER IS ONE WHO KNOWS THE WAY, GOES THE WAY, AND SHOWS THE WAY."

JOHN MAXWELL

5 Support

After 15+ years of holding a Fortune 500 corporate position, I had been given numerous examples of care. But I was restless only receiving. It felt like time to give back. I knew it was time for a change in my position. I decided to leave, shifting towards an unexpected career path of higher education. The decision raised eyebrows and sparked tense conversations. Those who knew me wanted to understand why I chose to abandon a successful corporate career. I found it difficult to explain. For me, that change wasn't about a job or pined-after title that I could hang on a door to a fancy office.

Instead, I yearned for significance. I needed a chance to make a tangible difference. I hungered to be part of a team who appreciated the unique value I brought to the organization. For me, I found that within a university setting. I admit, however, that I didn't recognize this was what I was looking for until I met a woman who would forge a path for me to find a way to leave a legacy.

In the midst of my career shift, Dr. Cathy entered my life. Or I should say—I entered her classroom.

A nearby campus had several open teaching positions. Intrigued by the prospect, when I inquired about one position, the school invited me to observe a lecture and engage with the professor afterward. As I sat outside room 101 before class, my attention was drawn to a poised and confident figure who walked down the hall.

In a perfectly tailored, navy blue suit, Dr. Cathy approached and invited me into her class. Her entrance was both impactful and a tad intimidating. She left a lasting impression on me during her lecture and in how she conducted herself with each student before and after class. In a single encounter, she inspired me to pursue a similar path. What I witnessed gave me a model to follow.

What I did not know that day was that Dr. Cathy wasn't just a professor; she was the Dean of the School of Business. As such, we had numerous conversations and interviews beyond our first introduction outside room 101. Throughout the vetting process, I continued to grow in confidence that my choice to leave the corporate world and pursue a path within education was right for me.

As I continued, my journey led me to a moment with Dr. Cathy, just prior to her offering me an instructor position.

Before sealing the deal, she leaned in to ask me a crucial question: "If I guide you to launch a career in higher education, will you commit to give back to others in the same way I am supporting you?"

I remember taking a moment. I knew her unconventional question deserved the dignity of making a calculated choice. "Can you promise me this?" She continued. In doing so, she already was coaching me. Her question was a challenge, a call to pay forward the opportunities and support that she was committing to provide to me.

After careful consideration, I responded with a resounding, "Yes, ma'am." From that moment on, her question became a daily part of

Chapter 5 - Support

my career. I made it a point to contribute to the development and support of others in my field. I saw it as my due diligence to share the knowledge, experience, mentorship and support she gave me outwards to my community. Her first challenge to me was not the last—as she remained an integral part of my career for several years.

Dr. Cathy not only set high standards for me, but also maintained her role as a mentor who cared deeply about me as an individual. Her support went beyond my immediate abilities; she cultivated impact by showing me the difference I could make within higher education. She was a leader who invested deeply in me and expected me to do the same for others. Rising to meet the challenges she set out for me was fulfilling and developing—something I know I was fortunate and blessed to receive. And her impact went beyond that portion of my career. To this day, she continues to invest in my growth and development—even though I am not currently at the same campus.

To me, her legacy in my life embodies what Support means—and exemplifies our final discussion point within the **CARES** framework.

As we define the **CARES** model, we discover that the "S" stands for Support. It signifies what it means to embrace a dedication to develop potential within a team. By actively seeking opportunities to enhance their training and foster their growth, support gives us a way to nurture emerging leaders who connect, acknowledge, respect, and empower others.

Cultivating a supportive environment is what forges a cycle of legacy.

Dr. Cathy's challenge to me to "give back" fits into this guiding principle of support. It also echoes John Maxwell's wisdom that a leader is one who knows the way, goes the way, and shows the way.[20] Support is a full circle approach, which allows care to scale within your organization. Such a supportive leadership philosophy focuses on giving others the tools they need to succeed, thus leaving a legacy of mentorship—sending care out to every corner of your organization.

SUPPORTIVE LEADERSHIP DEFINED

Have you ever met a leader who is under the impression that their leadership is centered on them? Have you ever worked for someone with this mindset? Many of us have met this type of manager—and few of us have thrived under them. *But why is that?* I find it is because this perspective limits them. They are unable to recognize the unrealized potential that exists within their team.

Instead, they are blinded by a base motivation to ensure that all accept their position of power. Thus, they fail to recognize the greatness, skill, and talent around them. They miss the fact that direct reports are capable of a great deal more than they know. Therefore, the organization suffers. Underutilized and under-valued employees may hope for change, yet eventually seek employment which allows them to thrive. After all, each of us longs to be acknowledged and valued for our contributions, versus being seen as a small part of a larger system.

On the other hand, "supportive leadership"—a concept from the Path-Goal Leadership Theory developed by Robert J. House[21]—is a way to weave a transformative approach into any organization. The Path-Goal Theory emphasizes the need for leaders to clarify the paths for direct reports to achieve their goals.

Supportive leaders are distinguished by approachability, empathy, and consideration for their team members' needs. They provide more than just emotional support. They work hard to foster a positive work environment in which everyone's skills are utilized. In stark contrast to power-dominant leaders, supportive leaders

Chapter 5 - Support

recognize and unlock unrealized potential within each member of their team. They view leadership as a way to provide autonomy and essential resources for independent work, ensuring each team member has the right set of tools to be equipped for success.

Irrespective of the team size, be it a group of 5 or 500, adopting a supportive leadership approach significantly elevates morale and champions for employees to achieve organizational goals. To begin adopting this mindset, we will explore the following seven traits commonly found in supportive leaders.

Take a moment to assess how you can up-level the way in which you embody each trait:

1.   Listen With Intent:

To do so, we must actively take part in processing, understanding, reacting to, and hearing what other people have to say. This trait requires us to pay full attention to the information which is shared with us, seek clarity, and show genuine interest in what others are saying.

2.   Help People To Solve Their Own Problems:

To do so, we must encourage team members to find and fix problems on their own. This does not mean we leave them stranded to solve issues in a silo. Instead, it requires us to give our team members the information, confidence, and tools they need to solve their own problems. Once accomplished, their victory builds their sense of independence and autonomy.

3.   Look For Ideas:

To do so, we must value the thoughts and opinions of team members by actively seeking their feedback. Adopting this trait means we recognize how different points of view help us to make decisions that are more holistic.

4. Give An Explanation:

To do so, we must provide clear reasoning for choices we make, or actions taken. This trait promotes transparency, while also sharing your logical thought process—giving others a chance to understand your leadership style. Such insight allows for feedback, but more importantly, grants an understanding as to why different decisions are being made within your business.

5. Acknowledge:

To do so, we must go beyond a simple pat on the back. Positive feedback demonstrates the fact that you notice and appreciate the work and accomplishments of your team members. This trait cultivates an environment which is supportive and inspiring. In turn, this creates loyalty as employees sense your gratitude and support.

6. Provide Information About The Company:

To do so, we must verbalize useful details about the group's objectives, beliefs, and direction. In doing so, we paint the picture of how each person's current actions are contributing to the overall vision and big-picture goals of the company. This trait helps team members to value each other's goals, and keep work aligned with the organization's overall objectives.

7. Share About Yourself:

To do so, we must be honest and open about our own feelings, experiences, and beliefs. This is not always easy. It requires a delicate balance of personal transparency, while still maintaining appropriate discussions within the professional world. But striving

Chapter 5 - Support

for that balance is crucial. Building trust happens in this zone. And trust is what makes a workplace cohesive, personable, and enjoyable.

Dr. Cathy embodied these seven qualities. She demonstrated what it meant to incorporate supportive leadership into her professional poise. Her unwavering support and mentorship were instrumental to me during my career transition. Her example set the tone for me to experience a positive and empowering work environment.

This continued for several years until she challenged me once more. She chose to leave the university. But before she did, I was presented with the opportunity to be promoted to Chair of the Business Department. Yet, I was reluctant to take it. She took one last "bet" on me—and asked me to continue to challenge myself. She accomplished this all while positioning me to be in a role which would allow me to provide the same supportive leadership she had demonstrated for me for years.

It was time to give back.

Dr. Cathy's approach to leading me, characterized by these seven traits, not only guided me personally but also gave space for each of my direct reports to be engaged and successful. Because of that, our department thrived even after her exit. Her exemplary approach transformed us into supportive leaders who were challenged to continue cultivating a thriving and motivated workforce.

THE POWER OF YOUR WORDS

Your words have power. They can change any atmosphere you are part of, including at work and any place your team gathers. Your words can leave others inspired, motivated, and positively challenged. Conversely, using negative or harmful language strips others of motivation, creates confusion, and demoralizes the team.

Supportive leaders recognize the power of their words. They are aware that tonality and word choice can have a big effect on their team members. Therefore, Supporting Leaders strive to use language in a way in which everyone on the team feels heard and valued. This occurs by verbally recognizing individual accomplishments, verbally valuing different points of view, and verbally promoting a positive environment. This language, in turn, allows people to feel like they fit and motivates them to offer their best at work.

Additionally, the way a leader verbalizes intentionally and goals sets the tone of trust needed in collaboration. Building trust will always start with clear communication. To do so means setting standards and providing insightful feedback. Such transparency encourages a culture of honesty and ethics—allowing team members the ability to stay focused on the task at hand, versus "watching their back."

Language is key. It is how leaders share goals, beliefs, and expectations. Communicating a clear vision grants everyone the ability to work toward the same goal. As supportive leaders discuss matters at hand with empathy and understanding, they build strong relationships. Thus, supportive language goes beyond conveying goals; it uplifts and inspires team members.

Curious where to begin to create a positive and thriving work environment? Consider the following examples of supportive language:

- I appreciate your perspective. Can you tell me more about your experience?
- Your input is valuable. Would you mind sharing your perspective on this matter?
- I trust your judgment. What solutions do you think would work best in this situation?

Chapter 5 - Support

- I believe in your ability to handle this challenge. How can I assist you in finding a solution?
- I value your intuition. What roadblocks do you think might happen on this project?
- I'd like to hear everyone's perspective. What input do you have to share?
- Let me explain the reasoning behind this decision. It's important for everyone to understand our approach, so I would like to share our logic in why we are taking this course of action. Feel free to provide feedback, we will have time for that at the end.
- I want to ensure clarity. Therefore, I want to talk about why we're taking this particular course of action.
- Great job on the project! Your dedication and hard work haven't gone unnoticed. I am especially grateful to ___ for ___ because that contribution allowed us to ___.
- I believe in your abilities. Keep up the excellent work; you're making a significant impact. Here is what we have heard from our clients…
- I want to keep you informed about our goals and direction as a company. Here's an update on our objectives and how they might impact you this quarter.
- Understanding our organizational values is crucial. Let's discuss how they align with our department's objectives.
- I'd like to know you better and share a bit about me. Let's have an open conversation about our experiences and perspectives.
- Transparency is important to me. Feel free to ask about my background. I value each of us being able to share our stories.

The way a leader talks shapes the culture of the company. Opening a door with intentional language can help leaders to cultivate an environment in which authentic engagement happens. In such a workspace, people are free to be creative, work in alignment, and offer their best to each other by carefully selecting the language they use. Directives are important, but so is the way they are delivered. How a leader communicates has the power to create teams of support, or to destroy it.

Language is often the distinction between the two.

THE CHALLENGES

Practicing supportive leadership is highly beneficial, but it is not without a set of specific challenges. In order to navigate what it means to be a supportive leader, we must unpack those challenges and overcome them.

These include:

Challenge #1 - Time Constraints:

To be a supportive leader, it takes time to actively listen, give insightful feedback, and have meaningful conversations with team members. Leaders will find it difficult to fit these objectives in when considering their other duties and time constraints.

Strategy To Overcome:

- Leaders can overcome time constraints with task prioritization, time management strategies, and delegation.

Challenge # 2 - Balancing Empathy And Objectivity:

It is difficult to find the right balance between empathy and objectivity. Leaders must be understanding and supportive, while also being able to make choices that are fair and in line with the organization's goals.

Chapter 5 - Support

Strategy To Overcome:

- Balancing empathy and objectivity is possible with clear guidelines, consultation with colleagues, regular self-reflection, and participation in training programs.

Challenge # 3 - Individual Differences:

Each individual has different wants, needs, and a way of working. Customizing support for each person requires a deep understanding of what makes them unique. This proves difficult when overseeing a larger group.

Strategy To Overcome:

- Address individual differences through regular check-ins. This can be accomplished by fostering open feedback, utilizing personality assessments, and maintaining flexibility in leadership styles.

Challenge # 4 - Maintaining Boundaries:

Leaders need to be supportive, while keeping professional limits. To avoid the problems which occur in overly casual leadership styles, it's important to find the right mix between being friendly and authoritative.

Strategy To Overcome:

- To maintain boundaries, leaders must establish clear policies, maintain role awareness, undergo regular training, and encourage peer accountability.

Challenge # 5 - Consistency:

Remaining supportive in constantly varying scenarios is not easy. Some leaders may find it difficult to stay helpful in high-pressure seasons.

Strategy To Overcome:

- Consistency can be achieved through routine practices, stress management, transparent communication, and by prioritizing self-care.

THE NEED FOR SUPPORTIVE LEADERSHIP

Recent research from McKinsey & Co emphasizes the importance of cultivating a positive environment via supportive leadership. According to their findings, organizations who foster an atmosphere in which employees feel comfortable asking for assistance, sharing informal suggestions, and challenging existing norms without the fear of negative social repercussions are in high demand.[22] Additionally, these companies are prone to innovation, harness the advantages of diversity, and exhibit adaptability to change. But creating such an organization takes work—and at the helm are supportive leaders.

Aligning with McKinsey & Co, we see that supportive leaders play a pivotal role in creating these high caliber environments. By prioritizing workplace mental health and adopting a supportive style, they not only elevate job satisfaction but also contribute to a culture that employees value. Their open communication and collaborative problem-solving prove to be essential elements which

Chapter 5 - Support

foster innovation, embrace diversity, and promote psychological safety.

In order to **CARE**—we must include psychological safety in our workspaces. Dr. Cathy demonstrated care towards me in how she challenged me. The key is to create an environment in which leaders go above and beyond their traditional roles of authority to give support for team members—both as professionals and individuals with their own needs.

Dr. Cathy modeled this philosophy in how she cared for the person behind the employee. By putting her team members' health and growth first, she not only created a good work environment, she also allowed each of us to feel psychologically safe. This promoted open communication, let us share our thoughts without worrying about repercussions, and granted us an advantage when it came to collaborating.

In terms of psychological safety, McKinsey & Company discovered that it is not enough for leaders to show support; they must strive to make the environment positive.[23] This occurs as team members are cared for as unique people, not just as employees. Such a holistic method ripples beyond making people feel safe; it sets off a chain reaction in which team members reciprocate, naturally supporting one other.

At the heart of this endeavor, accepting and celebrating each person's uniqueness proves key to supportive leadership. It creates a close-knit and trusted workplace, while building a collaborative team in which helping each other becomes second nature. As a result, goals and objectives are met from the improved performance and dynamics that the entire team has built together.

KEYS TO DEVELOP SUPPORTIVE LEADERSHIP

McKinsey's study underscores four key behaviors that leaders must embody in order to establish a supportive and psychologically safe environment.

These behaviors include:

- Open dialogue skills
- High-quality social relationships
- Situational humility
- Sponsorship[24]

Let's unpack each key, and process how we can cultivate each behavior into our leadership style:

KEY #1 - DEVELOPING OPEN DIALOGUE SKILLS

Actively Listen:

Leaders help their teams learn how to have open conversations each time they actively listen to them. To do so means paying full attention, paraphrasing for clarity to make sure you understand, and reacting in an appropriate way.

Train For Effective Communication:

Communication classes and training programs are efficient tools to help leaders improve their communication skills. By adopting these learning objectives, it is natural for leaders to get their points across and have complete conversations.

Chapter 5 - Support

Conflict-Resolution Workshops:

Learning how to settle disagreements in a constructive way is a skill which gives leaders tools to maintain an environment in which team members are safe to have open conversations.

KEY #2 - DEVELOPING HIGH-QUALITY SOCIAL RELATIONSHIPS

Team-Building Activities: Leaders who plan team-building workshops, activities, or retreats allow team members to know each other better—thus advocating for care. Such support promotes a happy, collaborative environment.

Inclusivity Training:

Leaders have a responsibility to make the workplace a space in which everyone feels as if they belong, regardless of identity or background. This is fostered through diversity and inclusiveness training. By sharing perspectives in an open environment, leaders build strong social relationships within the team.

Regular Check-Ins:

Leaders build connection on a personal level by setting up regular one-on-one or team check-ins. This builds relationships and friendships outside of task management or productivity requests.

KEY #3 - DEVELOPING SITUATIONAL HUMILITY

Feedback Seeking Culture:

Leaders create a culture of transparency and openness when they ask for and give feedback. Normalizing this practice helps leaders to stay humble by receiving input on where they can improve.

Learning From Failed Attempts:

Leaders have an opportunity to develop situational humility by viewing failed attempts as a chance to learn. To do so, means owning up to mistakes, processing them, and making personal changes to improve in the future.

Cross-Functional Collaboration:

Leaders are uniquely positioned to be able to learn from a range of points of view as they work with team members of all perspectives and backgrounds. Such cross-functional collaboration elevates and improves understanding.

KEY #4 – DEVELOPING SPONSORSHIP:

Setting Up Mentorship Programs:

Leaders who establish mentorship programs pair experienced workers with junior team members, thus keeping a wealth of knowledge and company practices embedded into company culture. Additionally, such internal partnerships put the onus of development on each team member's shoulders. The culture of care ripples through each department as senior members help and advise employees on their job development.

For Career Growth:

Leaders must actively champion for the career growth of their team members. This is fostered by providing projects, task ownership, or extra initiatives that will help them reach their professional goals—all while offering them support and resources as they take on new challenges.

Chapter 5 - Support

Networking Chances:

Leaders accelerate their team members' growth by providing opportunities for them to attend professional events—thus granting them access to innovative ideas and new professional connections.

Altogether, the cultivation of these behaviors transforms leaders, providing them with essential tools to build a positive, flourishing work environment. I recognize that some of these behaviors will come more naturally to you than others. Keep operating in your strengths—but also challenge yourself in the areas which do not come as easily.

Supportive leadership is a personal and evolving quest. It goes beyond acquiring skills. Instead, it's a commitment to value open communication, strong interpersonal connections, humility, and professional growth. As each of us challenge ourselves, this transformative process empowers us to instill a culture that promotes the well-being and success of every team member. In turn, our legacy of care means we have uplevel our own team by developing each one into a supportive leader who can answer the question: "Who cares?" with a resounding, "We do—and here is why."

PUT IT IN ACTION
SUPPORTIVE LEADERSHIP ACTION PLAN

How To Foster A Positive Team Environment In Your Organization

Instructions:

Use this worksheet to define specific objectives and action steps which will enhance supportive leadership skills within your team. Create your own actionable goals which give you a plan to develop each member of your team.

Who Cares?

FOSTERING OPEN DIALOGUE

Goal: To cultivate an environment in which open dialogue is valued.

Objective:

_____
_____
_____
_____
_____
_____

Action Steps:

_____
_____
_____
_____
_____
_____
_____

Questions For Reflection:

- How can you establish a feedback-friendly culture within your team?
- This week, what opportunities do you have to encourage team members to share ideas and concerns openly?
- How regularly do you schedule informal check-ins in which to foster open dialogue?

Chapter 5 - Support

DEVELOPING HIGH-QUALITY SOCIAL RELATIONSHIPS

Goal: To strengthen team bonds through social interactions.

Objective:

_____
_____
_____
_____
_____
_____
_____

Action Steps:

_____
_____
_____
_____
_____
_____
_____
_____
_____

Question For Reflection:

- What team-building activities can you organize this month in order to enhance social connection?
- What diversity training could you initiate this quarter? How do you see it fostering inclusivity within the team?
- This week, what can you do to initiate casual, non-work-related team gatherings to build camaraderie?

Who Cares?

DEVELOPING SITUATIONAL HUMILITY

Goal: To cultivate humility in leadership.

Objective:

_____
_____
_____
_____
_____
_____
_____

Action Steps:

_____
_____
_____
_____
_____
_____
_____
_____

Question For Reflection:

- How frequently do you seek feedback from team members?
- What does embracing a learning mindset look like for you when you face a challenging situation?
- How comfortable are you in sharing personal experiences and lessons learned? How does this practice cultivate your sense of humility?

Chapter 5 - Support

SPONSORSHIP

Goal: To actively support team members' career growth.

Objective:

_____
_____
_____
_____
_____
_____
_____

Action Steps:

_____
_____
_____
_____
_____
_____
_____
_____

Question For Reflection:

- What mentorship programs can you establish to support the career development of your team?
- This week, how can you invite team members' participation in projects which align with their professional goals?
- What networking opportunities exist which would support your team's professional growth?

Who Cares?

Chapter 5 - Support

PEOPLE DON'T CARE HOW MUCH YOU KNOW,
UNTIL THEY KNOW HOW MUCH YOU CARE.

JOHN MAXWELL

Conclusion

As we near the end of our journey through the pages of the **CARES** book, I find myself profoundly impacted by the principles it embodies: Connection, Acknowledgment, Respect, Empowerment, and Support. Throughout our exploration, we've delved into these foundational pillars of compassionate leadership and uncovered the truths that guide us towards creating a more empathetic and supportive world.

One of the most striking revelations has been the recognition of the profound interconnectedness among all humanity. We are not isolated individuals navigating life's challenges alone; rather, we are interconnected beings, each thread woven into the fabric of society, reliant on the strength and support of one another. As a **CARES** leader, I've come to realize that fostering meaningful connections is not merely a strategy for success but an essential aspect of our shared existence. By nurturing these connections, we amplify our strengths, compensate for our weaknesses, and cultivate bonds that transcend individual pursuits.

Acknowledgment has emerged as another cornerstone of effective leadership within the **CARES** framework. In a world constantly evolving, the ability to recognize and adapt to the diverse perspectives and experiences of others is paramount. The lessons gleaned from our exploration underscore the importance of remaining open-minded, flexible, and resilient in the face of adversity. It's about embracing the fluidity of life and seizing opportunities for growth and innovation.

Respect remains at the core of **CARES** leadership. In a society marked by division and discord, cultivating a culture of mutual respect is more crucial than ever. Regardless of differences in background, beliefs, or perspectives, every individual deserves to be treated with dignity and kindness. By fostering an environment of inclusivity and acceptance, we create spaces where everyone feels valued and empowered to contribute their unique talents and insights.

Empowerment, perhaps, is the most transformative aspect of **CARES** leadership. The ability to uplift and empower those around us is a hallmark of compassionate leadership. Through the pages of the book, I've learned that empowerment is not just about offering a helping hand; it's about providing the tools, resources, and support necessary for individuals to thrive and reach their full potential.

Lastly, but certainly not least, is the principle of support. As **CARES** leaders, it is our duty to be a source of strength and encouragement for those around us. Whether it's offering a listening ear, extending a helping hand, or providing guidance and mentorship, the support we offer can have a profound impact, extending far beyond what we can imagine.

So, as we conclude our journey through the **CARES** book, I want to leave you with this: I believe in you. I believe in the transformative power of **CARES** leadership to create positive change in the world. We've outlined action items, discussed next steps, but now it's time to embody the principles we've learned. Let's not just talk about Connection, Acknowledgment, Respect, Empowerment, and Support – let's live them out in everything we do.

Conclusion

Together, let's create a world where compassion reigns supreme, where every individual feels seen, heard, and valued. The journey begins now.

ABOUT THE AUTHOR

With two decades of extensive leadership experience spanning both corporate and academic realms, Dr. Lynn Johnson stands as a beacon of innovation and excellence in the fields of human resource management and education.

In 2019, Dr. Lynn took her passion for organizational excellence to new heights by founding Triumphant HR Solutions. Through this visionary venture, she offers a comprehensive suite of services tailored to small to medium-sized for-profit and nonprofit organizations. Dr. Lynn's approach is marked by close collaboration with clients, as she diligently identifies optimal strategies for enhancing organizational performance and fostering a culture of excellence. Her goal? To create nothing short of the "best places to work" where skilled and dedicated staff flourish.

Specializing in leadership, employee engagement diversity, equity, and inclusion (DEI), Dr. Lynn's expertise extends far beyond the boardroom. As an adjunct faculty member at various universities, she seamlessly integrates practical insights from the field of Human Resource Management into both undergraduate and graduate curricula, enriching the academic landscape and shaping the future leaders of tomorrow.

Not content with her impact solely within the classroom, Dr. Lynn extends her influence to the Greater Orlando Society for Human Resource Management (GOSHRM) Chapter, where she serves as President-Elect. Her dedication to advancing the HR profession at a local level is a testament to her commitment to continuous improvement and excellence. In 2025, she will ascend to the presidency, further solidifying her role as a trailblazer in her field.

A sought-after keynote speaker, Dr. Lynn captivates audiences with her dynamic presentations, empowering them with actionable tools for catalyzing transformative change. Her ability to inspire shifts in mindset and foster lasting behavioral changes is unparalleled, leaving a profound impact on all who have the privilege of hearing her speak.

Dr. Lynn Johnson's unwavering commitment to nurturing talent, fostering effective leadership, and championing diversity and inclusion in workplaces is not just a career choice—it's a calling. Her lasting impact in the field is a testament to her tireless dedication and passion for creating positive change wherever she goes.

You can connect with Dr. Lynn at:

www.IamDrLynn.com

ACKNOWLEDGMENTS

Writing a book is not a solitary endeavor; it takes a village of support, encouragement, and inspiration. As I reflect on the journey of creating *Who Cares*; I am deeply grateful to the following individuals:

To Cassandra Smith, my editor, whose arrival in my life was luck by chance. Your expertise, patience, and encouragement were instrumental in transforming the countless ideas in my mind into words on paper. Your guidance made this project possible in ways you may never fully comprehend.

To my friends and family, who stood by me with unwavering support and enthusiasm. Your cheers and listening ears during both the triumphs and challenges of writing this book meant the world to me. Your belief in me fueled my determination to see this project through to fruition.

To the countless leaders whose wisdom and insights served as the foundation for *Who Cares*. Your expertise and experiences provided invaluable perspectives that enriched the pages of this book. I am indebted to each of you for sharing your knowledge and shaping the narrative of this work.

To my beloved husband, LyVonski, and my children and grandchildren, your understanding and patience throughout this endeavor were truly remarkable. Your unwavering support and love sustained me through the demanding moments of writing.

I dedicate this book to you as a testament to the limitless potential that resides within each of you. Carter Lynn, Riley Rae, and Kamry Luella, may this book serve as a reminder that you can achieve anything you set your minds to. I aspire to be an example for you, and I am profoundly grateful for the love and inspiration you bring into my life.

ENDNOTES

1. Gallup. (2022, August 17). Percent Who Feel Employer Cares About Well-Being Plummets. Retrieved from https://www.gallup.com/workplace/390776/percent-feel-employer-cares-wellbeing-plummets.aspx

2. MIT Sloan Review. (2022, August). Mental Health Has Become a Business Imperative. Retrieved from https://sloanreview.mit.edu/article/mental-health-has-become-a-business-imperative/?utm_source=linkedin&utm_medium=social&utm_campaign=sm-direct

3. MIT Sloan Review. (2022, August). Mental Health Has Become a Business Imperative. Retrieved from https://sloanreview.mit.edu/article/mental-health-has-become-a-business-imperative/?utm_source=linkedin&utm_medium=social&utm_campaign=sm-direct

4. Brower, T. (2023, January 29). Managers have major impact on mental health: How to lead for wellbeing. Forbes. https://www.forbes.com/sites/tracybrower/2023/01/29/managers-have-major-impact-on-mental-health-how-to-lead-for-wellbeing/?sh=3f04eb172ec1

5. UKG. (2023, January). Managers impact our mental health more than doctors, therapists, and same spouses. Retrieved from https://www.ukg.com/about-us/newsroom/managers-impact-our-mental-health-more-doctors-therapists-and-same-spouses#:~:text=Managers%20impact%20employees'%20mental%20health,than%20a%20high%2Dpaying%20job.

6. Brodey, D. (2021, June 21). 93% of managers watch as mental health negatively impacts bottom line. Forbes. Retrieved from https://www.forbes.com/sites/denisebrodey/2021/06/21/93-of-managers-watch-as-mental-health-negatively-impacts-bottom-line/?sh=5b3d29771bf9

7. Gallup. (2018, January). Why We Need Best Friends at Work. Retrieved from https://www.gallup.com/workplace/236213/why-need-best-friends-work.aspx

8. Eagle Hill Consulting. (2023, January). Fostering employee connection beyond relationships delivers big business results. Retrieved from https://www.eaglehillconsulting.com/insights/employee-connection/

9. PR Newswire. (2022, October). Enboarder Research Reveals the Value of Human Connection in the Workplace. Retrieved from https://www.prnewswire.com/news-releases/enboarder-research-reveals-the-value-of-human-connection-in-the-workplace-301645170.html

10. Maslow, A. H. (1943). A Theory of Human Motivation. Psychological Review, 50(4), 370-396. Retrieved from https://www.semanticscholar.org/paper/A-Theory-of-Human-Motivation-Maslow/06754f2bc0564b83af01b220b15a574e0adef883

11. Robinson, B. (2023, January 6). 4 Ways Workplace Leaders Can Create a Culture of Connection in 2023. Forbes. Retrieved from https://www.forbes.com/sites/bryanrobinson/2023/01/06/4-ways-workplace-leaders-can-create-a-culture-of-connection-in-2023/?sh=354f7e376db5

12. McKinsey & Company. (2021, September). Great Attrition or Great Attraction: The Choice is Yours. Retrieved from https://www.mckinsey.com/capabilities/people-and-organizational-performance/our-insights/great-attrition-or-great-attraction-the-choice-is-yours

13. Harvard Gazette. (2013, May). Winfrey's Commencement Address. Retrieved from https://news.harvard.edu/gazette/story/2013/05/winfreys-commencement-address/

14. Harvard Business School Publishing. (2021, May). Research: What do people need to perform at a High Level. Retrieved from https://hbsp.harvard.edu/download?url=%2Fcatalog%2Fsample%2FH06BYY-PDF-ENG%2Fcontent&metadata=e30%3D

15. Westfall, C. (2022, March 4). The Importance of Acknowledgment: How Empathy Drives Leadership. Forbes. Retrieved from https://www.forbes.com/sites/chriswestfall/2022/03/04/the-importance-of-acknowledgment-how-empathy-drives-leadership/?sh=5180c532329b

16. Rogers, K. (2018, July). Do Your Employees Feel Respected? Harvard Business Review. Retrieved from https://hbr.org/2018/07/do-your-employees-feel-respected

17. Hewlin, P. F., Kim, S. S., & Song, Y. H. (2016). Creating facades of conformity in the face of job insecurity: A study of consequences and conditions. Journal of Occupational & Organizational Psychology, 89(3), 539–567 https://doi.org/10.1111/joop.12140

18. Inclusive Leadership. (2021). The Importance of Authenticity in the Workplace. Retrieved from https://www.inclusiveleadership.com/wp-content/uploads/2021/07/The-Importance-of-Authenticity-in-the-Workplace.pdf

19. Inclusive Leadership. (2021). The Importance of Authenticity in the Workplace. Retrieved from https://www.inclusiveleadership.com/wp-content/uploads/2021/07/The-Importance-of-Authenticity-in-the-Workplace.pdf

20. Life Wisdom: Quotes from John Maxwell: Insights on Leadership. (2014, May 1).Hardcover.

21. House, R. J. (1971). A path-goal theory of leader effectiveness. Administrative Science Quarterly, 16, 321-338.

22. McKinsey & Company. (2022, February). Psychological Safety and the Critical Role of Leadership Development. Retrieved from https://www.mckinsey.com/capabilities/people-and-organizational-performance/our-insights/psychological-safety-and-the-critical-role-of-leadership-development

23. McKinsey & Company. (2022, February). Psychological Safety and the Critical Role of Leadership Development. Retrieved from https://www.mckinsey.com/capabilities/people-and-organizational-performance/our-insights/psychological-safety-and-the-critical-role-of-leadership-development

24. McKinsey & Company. (2022, February). Psychological Safety and the Critical Role of Leadership Development. Retrieved from https://www.mckinsey.com/capabilities/people-and-organizational-performance/our-insights/psychological-safety-and-the-critical-role-of-leadership-development

Made in the USA
Middletown, DE
21 July 2024

57479608R00096